I0453241

Memoirs of a Soldier and an Ambassador for Christ

Original Edition - Includes Early Life Reflections on Race and Faith

Lloyd C. Glover

- Hardcover Edition: 979-8-9931039-4-5
- Paperback Edition: 979-8-9931039-5-2
- Revised Paperback Edition: 979-8-9931039-0-7
- Revised eBook Edition: 979-8-9931039-1-4
- Original eBook Edition: 979-8-9931039-2-1
- Audiobook Edition ASIN: B0CHN9TFGD
* Library of Congress Control Number: 2025920618

- Original Edition — Includes chapters detailing the author's early life growing up as a Negro in America.
- Revised Edition — Focuses more directly on the author's military service and spiritual transformation.

Printed in the United States of America

Table of Contents

Dedication

I dedicate this book to the memory of my mother Eva Joan Glover for her inspiration and love and to my wife Tammy and to all the military spouses that are unsung heroes in support of their loved ones that deployed to foreign wars. You are heroes too.

Special Thanks

To Jane Thoner, Librarian, Plainfield Public Library, Plainfield, New Jersey for her research of historical information that help me in the completion of my memoirs.

Thank you.

The Beginning of My Story

It is my pleasure to introduce myself to you as Lloyd Calvin Glover. I am a soldier and an ambassador for Christ. The Bible says that every Christian has been given a measure of faith and is an ambassador for Christ. Every one of us has been given something special that God wants us to do for His kingdom and to share with others about His goodness, grace, and mercy. Now that I am older, much wiser, and full of faith, I can look back at the history of my life and recount how my childhood growing up as a young Negro kid in America was awakened by the racial tensions of the sixties and seventies; affected by the events of the Vietnam War; and strengthened by my participation as a Christian soldier in the Gulf War, serving in the defense of the nation of Israel and, a year later, serving in the defense of the Kingdom of Saudi Arabia, and then my life in ministry after my retirement from the United States Army.

The Holy Spirit has appointed me to say that every airmen, coast guardsman, Marine, sailor, soldier, and government worker who is a true believer in Christ and does the will of the Father and who is serving or has served our great nation to the glory of God and doing his or her part in the advancement of God's kingdom is also a representative and an ambassador for Christ. It does not matter if you are just a new believer, choir member, Sunday school teacher, or someone leading a ministry. We all have our part to play in the advancement of God's kingdom. God is no respecter of persons. I cherish the fact that God is not only the author and finisher of my faith, but also the Commander of my salvation and my life. I knew when I was ten that my steps have been ordered and protected by God. The spirit in me knew that I was going to join the military. I also understood spiritually that this was the career path that God had chosen for me. God allowed me to make the decision to either serve in the Army or the Marines. I was really leaning toward joining the Marines because of their beautiful uniforms and their proud history: however, I felt deep in my spirit that the Air Force, Army, Coast Guard, and Navy had a proud history in war and peace too. But the Army was the branch of service that I felt was perfect for me.

So, I chose the Army. It was early in my military career when I discovered, by the power of the Holy Spirit, that I could serve in the military and represent Christ at the same time no matter where I was stationed in the world. I felt the power of God that had anointed me to be both a soldier and an ambassador for Christ. The joy of knowing who I am in Christ and who I represented allowed me to be both an anointed soldier in God's army and a good soldier in the greatest army and country in the world. Both assignments I always did to the glory of God. Amen.

My life experiences, under the direction and guidance of the Holy Spirit, had increased my understanding and love for the body of Christ, the three Abrahamic religions, faith, humanity, and the nature of God. Once when I was praying in the spirit, I was bold enough to asked God two questions.

I asked God, "What did I do to deserve your amazing love, mercy, and grace?" and "Why did you choose me to be one of your representatives and ambassador for Christ?"

God responded to me in a gentle whisper to my spirit and said, "Lloyd, my son, because I Am that I Am. There is no other, because of my Son whom you have accepted as your Savior, who you call Jesus who paid it all on the cross at Calvary, and because I have loved you with an everlasting love even before you were a seed and soul planted in your mother's womb, and because I will have need of you, my son. You will see in due season the reason why We have chosen you."

I cried, spoke in tongues, and lay prostrated on the floor of my private space for what seemed like hours, realizing for the first time in my life that God, the God of all creation, spoke my name and that He Himself said that I was needed and chosen by Him, to do something for His kingdom in due season. Amen.

Every one of us has been given a unique assignment and story that God has purposely placed within our spirit. Your story, just like my story, can only be told by you. God has commissioned me with this anointed assignment to recount and share my story, which includes the good, the bad and the ugly experiences that I have encountered throughout my lifetime. Your story, just like my story, and those of our brothers and sisters that were Christ's first ambassadors of the early church had a story to tell that was passed down for generations to know and to enjoy. That is why Christianity is so rich in Bible history and why we have the Bible today and other Christian resource materials. Our stories, when written in books and shared with the world, is a testament and a sweet taste and an expression of the grace, mercy, saving power and the goodness and faithfulness of our God that we have experienced for ourselves. It is also a sweet sound to the hearing of God when it is read out loud.

Just like the first ambassadors of the early church and those brothers and sisters that were first called Christians at Antioch, and every believer of Christ since then down to the present-day believers, we all have something worth passing on about our relationship with God the Father, God the Son, and God the Holy Spirit. Our published words can be an everlasting testament about our life and love of God. Let our written words serve as proof that we were once here and that we had a Father-son or a Father-daughter relationship with our Creator. Let our written words be like that shiny star in the sky to the world and to our future generations that our lives did matter and that our journey with God was a divine truth worth sharing and shouting about. Our life lessons, when shared could be the catalyst that can save generations to come. I believe by faith that the Holy

Spirit is my coauthor that is guiding and inspiring my every thought as I write my life story. I pray that the treasures of my life story and what is contained in this book is a teaching tool to enhance the knowledge and love for the one who sits high and lifted up on His throne. Amen.

Let me take this opportunity to do what God has commissioned me to do by recounting and sharing my life story.

I grew up in a small town located in central New Jersey called Plainfield. I was only two years old when my parents, Sammy and Eva Joann Glover, fulfilled the American dream by buying their first home in May of 1960. The Johnson family was the first Negro family to move into this segregated middle-class neighborhood on the east side of town. My family was the second Negro family to settle into this neighborhood. We moved in a couple of days after the Johnsons family did. We moved in two houses down on the same side of the street from the Johnsons. It did not take long before my parents and the Johnsons became good friends and realized that several White families were starting to move out. I was too young at the time to know, but my mother told me years later that they suspected that those families that did move out of the neighborhood did so because they did not want to live in or to be known as a White family that lived in a neighborhood that had Negro families living among them.

Mom also said that it was like a chain reaction, as one White family moved out, one more Negro family moved in. The White families that stayed were known as good neighbors. Most of them were Christians that believed in God and believed in the Bible truth that we all were created by the same God and that we all were created equal. Those families that stayed became good neighbors and friends to our parents. Their children became our childhood and lifelong friends even to this day. One of those families that still live there today is the Mikla family. Our families have maintained our friendship through time.

We also have the pleasure of watching our sons and daughters and some of our grandkids growing up in this same neighborhood that raised us as kids. My youngest sister, Mary, was able to purchase our parents' home later in life. This kept our parents' dream alive that their treasured home would remain in the family after they were gone. Mary is living there today with her husband, Eric, and they are raising their youngest son, Marcellus, in her childhood home.

Sure, even back then, in our neighborhood, we had our share of fights and disagreements about various issues like some neighbors do; but none of these verbal fights or disagreements led to any physical fights, nor were they ever racially motivated. Just like good neighbors, we were able to work out our differences, and we were able to continue with our friendships. We all took pride in welcoming every new family that moved into our neighborhood with open arms regardless of their skin color, nationality, or religious preference.

My first thoughts and my desires to let God know how I felt about Him began November 23, 1963. A day that I can still remember all too well. The events that unfolded that afternoon on this tragic day not only affected my young life but affected the lives of the entire world. The day created a historical date that was recorded in the annals of American and world history.

On this day, I was a five-year-old kindergarten student sitting at my small wooden desk at Woodland Elementary School. Woodland had a morning and an afternoon kindergarten class. I was in the afternoon class. My kindergarten teacher's name was Mrs. Coward. She was genuinely nice and loved teaching her students. I enjoyed playing games, and I was a friend to every student in my classroom. We had just finished playing musical chairs and had just sat down at our assigned wooden desk when suddenly the telephone on the wall in our classroom began to ring. We all got silent, because the only time that the phone would ring is when someone was being sent home or someone was called down to the principal's office because they were in trouble. Mrs. Coward, my teacher, answered the telephone.

You could see the sadness that covered her face as she listened to the person speaking to her on the other end. I could tell by her facial expressions and by the tears that were starting to slowly stream from her eyes that something bad must have just happened. You could also hear the commotion of students in the hallway that sounded like they were preparing to leave the school. You could also hear the teachers that were standing near our classroom door that were talking among themselves. I could also remember hearing some of the teachers crying. Whatever it was, I thought to my young self, that it must had been bad enough because when Mrs. Coward hung up the telephone, she told us that we were being dismissed right away and that we needed to go straight home to our parents.

I really thought that the world was ending on this day because we were always practicing those scary air-raid drills. I once asked my father about these drills. He explained to me that the reason we practice so many of these drills is because the Russians were our enemy, they did not like Americans, and they could come and attack us any day. He also said that our principal, teachers, and our parents wanted to make sure that we were prepared in school by practicing so many of these drills just in case that the Russians did come to attack us.

I can still remember slowly walking home by myself on those lonely long two blocks from my school to my house. It was a five-minute walk, but today, it seemed longer. I kept on thinking, and I could still hear Dad's voice that was haunting my mind, about the fact that the Russians were coming. I was sad as I thought about my teacher, Mrs. Coward, and all my friends from school that I thought I would never see or play with again. Just as soon as I arrived home from school, I looked through our half-glass storm door. I could see Momma sitting in the front room with five or seven of our Negro neighbors. They were all gathered in front of our black-and-white television set watching the news. They were at our house because not every Negro family could afford their own TV set at the time. Everyone in the house was silent and sad. There was a few of the ladies that were weeping and wiping away their tears.

I opened the door and walked inside our house. Momma started talking to one of our lady neighbors about what was going on in the news. I tried to listen to what Momma was saying, but I could not because I did not want to appear like I was eavesdropping on her conversation with our neighbor. So, I had to wait a couple of minutes until she was finished speaking. I knew better not to eavesdrop or interrupt Momma while she was talking. I interrupted her twice before. The first time that I did it, she gave me a tongue-lashing and a warning. Momma made it a point to explain to me why I should never ever appear nosy or interrupt grown folks while they were talking. A couple of weeks ago I forgot and did it again for the second time. This time Momma was not so nice. She did not say a word. She backhanded me so fast and popped me so hard on my lips for interrupting her again. Boy! I did not like it, but the truth is, I learned my lesson the hard way.

When she finished speaking, Momma motioned to me to go into the kitchen. Momma told me to sit down at the table, and she began to explain to me in her caring motherly voice that President Kennedy, our president, was shot and killed by someone today. I was sad to hear this and sad for his family too, but I was also relieved that the world was not ending. I was happy and sad at the same time, so I went outside to find my best friend, Brian.

As I walked over to Brian's house, which was across the street on the corner, I noticed a lot of cars parked in front and on the side of his house. As soon as I knocked on Brian's door, a strange man with tears in his eyes opened the door and greeted me. He said with a husky voice, "Can I help you?" I remembered what Momma said about being nosy, but I was curious why the strange man answered the door with tears in his eyes, so I looked inside the house passed him and noticed that there were a lot of strange people that I never saw before in Brian's house. I could tell that there was something wrong. I thought that this was strange. There were several Negroes and White people with their eyes closed in a circle around Brian's mother, holding hands. There was another lady in the middle of the circle with Brian's mother. She was hugging and praying loudly so that everyone in the room could hear her. I asked the man if Brian could come out to play. The strange man told me nicely that Brian was not feeling well and that he could not come out to play today. So, I went and played with my other friends for a little while. I then went back home when Momma called me because it was time to eat dinner with my family.

Later that evening, Mom put me in the bathtub. She told me that she was going over to Brian's house to speak with Brian's mother. She also said that Dad was in the backyard playing horseshoes with his friends and that Sammy and Isaac were downstairs watching cartoons. Mom said that she would be right back. I finished taking my nighttime bath and put on my pajamas.

Twenty minutes later, Momma returned home from being over Brian's house. Mom came back and was sitting on the couch. She called me and my two brothers to come and sit down next to her. Momma had tears streaming from her eyes. She began to explain to us that Brian's father had died on this day too. He was killed earlier in the day in an automobile accident while going to work at his church. My mother knew Brian's father as a friend, a Christian pastor, community leader, and a good neighbor. Mom knew Brian was my best friend. She wanted to make sure

15

that we were aware and did not want us to say anything that would upset my best friend or Brian's older brother, David, who was a friend to my two older brothers, Sammy and Isaac. I realized then that this was the reason so many people were at Brian's house earlier today. This was the first time in my young life that I understood that people do die and that even good people that believed in God and trust in Him die too.

Even at the age of five, I knew that President Kennedy was our first Catholic president. This came from hearing what was always said about him on the television news. I thought about our president, a family man, a Catholic, and the most powerful man in the world, and my best friend's father, who I knew as Brian's father and a church pastor. They were men who believed and loved God, and both were killed on the same day. I questioned God about why this happened. He never did answer me. This was the beginning of my many talks with God and the beginning of my personal Father- son relationship with our Abba Father. Amen.

My Best Friend, Brian, and the Turbulent Sixties

My best friend, Brian, was a mixed kid. His father was a Negro pastor and his mother was a White schoolteacher at my school land Elementary. Brian's skin complexion and golden-brown curly textured hair would have easily convinced you that he was strictly a White kid. I thought that Brian was special because he was the only mixed kid that I knew at that time. Brian's mother was the nicest person in the world that I knew growing up. To be honest, I really did not know Brian's father all that well. It seemed like he was always gone to the church whenever I played over Brian's house. I played over Brian's house just about every day. Brian was my best friend and my blood brother too.

The next day Brian came outside and over to my house to play with me. We really did not play that much that day because Brian was sad. Because Brian was sad, it made me sad too. We sat on our back porch picking up rocks and throwing them back into our gravel driveway. We talked briefly about what had happened to his father. We both were angry at God and could not understand why God took his father to heaven so soon.

Brian and I, along with several other Negro and White kids in our neighborhood, would play Army all day and all around Brian's front yard and backyard. We were armed with our fake machine guns, rifles, and grenades. We used our voices to simulate the sounds of the guns firing and the sounds of the grenades exploding in the air and on the ground. We would also battle with our GI Joe toys and our plastic Army soldiers that we would move around and position with our hands for battle on a small dirt hill and sandbox in Brian's backyard. We would play so much that Brian's mother would come outside on the extremely hot days with peanut butter and jelly sandwiches and Kool-Aid with ice cubes to cool us down.

On some of the other days, it would be lemonade with cut-up lemons in the glasses.

She was the greatest mom and would function as our general. She would order us to come on their back porch to take a much- needed break from the hot sun. Being good soldiers, we did what our general ordered. We would then get in a single file in military formation and marched like soldiers on to the porch. We took the much-needed break from the sun, joked around for a little bit, then we would immediately return to playing army again. We had so much fun playing together back then. We called ourselves the Hillside-Berkman Street fighting soldiers. We all talked about being soldiers when we grow up.

Speaking of being a soldier, we had in our own neighborhood a former military officer. Mr. Warren Mark Henry lived across the street from my family. He was a second lieutenant in the Army Air Force during World War II. What made Mr. Henry so special was that he was a Negro pilot who flew cargo planes for the famous Tuskegee Airmen. The Tuskegee Airmen were mostly an all-Negro fighter pilots, bombers, and airmen unit that served our country honorably in World War II. Even though Second Lieutenant Henry did not go to war, he played a vital role in flying cargo planes in support of their war effort. Here is his listing from the Tuskegee pilot historical record:

Henry, Warren E. 44-H-TE 9/8/1944
2nd Lt. 0838037 Plainfield NJ. Plainfield.

I also found out later that Plainfield had two other famous Tuskegee airmen too; however, I did not know either of them. They are the following:

Black, Samuel A. 43-K-TE 12/5/1943
2nd Lt. 08 17595 Plainfield NJ

Carpenter, Russell W. 44-I-SE 11/20/1944 2nd Lt.
0839085 Plainfield NJ.

Mr. Henry was my first hero. I was proud of these Tuskegee airmen, and it is worth mentioning their achievement and service to
our country.

Tuskegee Airmen. Lieutenant Henry, first kneeling to the left

I often thought about how tough it must have been being a Negro pilot during World War II with all the harassments they had to go through by the White pilots. We also had three other Negro servicemen from my neighborhood that planted the seeds in my mind about joining the military when I graduate from high school: Mr. Jay Hall, who lived two houses down from me, was at that time an officer in the Army Reserve; Mr. Naaman Gray, who lived four houses down from me, was a master sergeant in the Air

Force Reserves; and my uncle Alfred Morris who lived across the street from me. He had recently retired from the Air Force as a master sergeant. I enjoyed talking to each of these men about their experience in the service. They all agreed on the same thing— joining the military would give me the necessary discipline to be successful and would be the best opportunity for me to get ahead in life. Each one of these brave heroes was proud to have served our country in war and peace. I was proud to have known all these men.

I was proud and loved seeing Mr. Hall and Mr. Gray in their military uniforms as they prepare to go to their monthly reserve drill meetings. I knew then that I wanted to serve my country like my four military heroes that I watched while I was growing up. Plainfield had a Memorial Day, Fourth of July, and a Veterans Day parade; and Brian and I would make it our mission to go downtown to see the parades. We would wave our small American handheld flags and cheer loudly for the military men and women as they march by or passed by on their floats or on their military vehicles. Every year Mr. Gray would take me and his son, Butch, to McGuire Air Force Base to see the air shows. It was amazing to see all the different aircrafts that were on display and those aircrafts that were doing fantastic acrobatic maneuvers in the air show.

The Army also had helicopters, tanks, weapons, and other equipment on display from Fort Dix Army base, which was next to the Air Force base. I was also impressed to see the Air Force and Army men and women walking around in their military uniforms. I noticed that the Army soldiers always had on starch uniforms and spit shine boots and really looked sharp, while the Air Force airmen uniforms were not as nice and their boots never shined. I think seeing the sharpness of the Army soldiers help me decide that I was going into the Army after high school.

The 1960s was a turbulent time in the United States. Malcolm X, a well-spoken Negro Muslim minister and a Civil Rights activist, was assassinated in 1965. Bobby Kennedy, a United States senator and the younger brother of the late President Kennedy, and Martin Luther King Jr., a famous Negro minister and a national leader in our Negro community were both assassinated in 1968. Martin Luther King Jr. spoke so elegantly about having a dream and was the same man that was always preaching about racial equality and always leading marches and peaceful protests. I asked my parents why they were killed. They could not explain to me why these good and godly men were killed. I was only ten years old when they were killed. I asked God the same question that I asked my parents because I wanted to know why.

The Vietnam War was raging on. Brian and I would always ride our bikes around our neighborhood. There was a funeral home that was on a main street a couple blocks away from our neighborhood that could easily be mistaken as a haunted house. It was located on one of the corners that we would pass by every day. It seemed like at least three times a week, especially around 11:00 a.m. on the dot, that a funeral service was being held. Some of these services were for servicemen killed in the Vietnam War. I remember seeing the flagged-draped caskets of the young men killed in the war that were returned home to their grieving families and friends. One of these funerals had the casket of a young teenage White soldier from our neighborhood who was also killed in the war. We were hurt and sad. I remember us looking at each other and asking God the question why he and so many other young men have to die in the war.

We would get off our bikes, stand at attention, salute with our right hand like soldiers do; and we would watch with pride as their caskets are ushered into the funeral home by military pallbearers. They would step in unison to the voice of the sergeant that was calling the marching steps as they marched in. Sometimes we stayed long enough

21

until the end as they marched out of the funeral home. Each time there were honor guards with their neatly pressed uniforms, black spit shine boots, rifles, and their shiny helmets that were posted outside the funeral home in honor of our fallen heroes.

There was also a father named Sergeant Jackson who was from our neighbor that was killed in the Vietnam War too. My sister Yvonne was a friend of his daughter. It was a sad day when we heard the news.

Riots were happening everywhere. Negro people were rioting and tearing up, to my lack of understanding, their own neighborhoods and looting their local stores because of what they believed were social injustices and inequality in the society, like the lack of affordable quality housing, the right to vote without intimidation, better jobs with better wages, the right to work, police brutality, and the anger at the perception of being looked down at or being classified as second-class citizens.

My hometown had a police officer named John Gleason. He was killed during the 1967 Plainfield riots.

The hippies and the flower children were protesting the war. There was Woodstock, which occurred in 1969 with the purpose of spreading unity and peace. Four hundred thousand young people from all around the United States went to California to camp out for three days at Woodstock to show their support for peace and for racial and gender equality, with the main goal about being heard to help end the Vietnam War.

I bet Brian a pinky bet that the hippies were at Woodstock and that Jimmy Hendrix was playing his guitar there too. I won the bet.

There were KKK rallies. The name of George Wallace and the fictitious name of Jim Crow were rallying calls for White supremacist that wanted to "make America great again," a similar code and rallying call used by our former president.

Black Muslims and the Black Panthers were everywhere trying to recruit young Negro teenage boys, men, and women for their services and for their movements too.

The war draft was going on. The less fortunate, mostly Negro young men and the White folks with less money, were being drafted for the war while the rich were staying in school if they could with the purpose of avoiding the war.

I also can remember that there were high school seniors from around my neighborhood that were purposely failing the one class that they needed to graduate from high school. They knew that failing this one important class prevented them from graduating and keeping them in high school and being ineligible for the draft. They remained high school seniors for three more years or until they reached the maximum school age of twenty-one. There were other ways that young Negros, White, Hispanic, Asian, rich, and poor men took to avoid the draft, like leaving family, friends, and home by going to Canada. They understood that they could never return home. They could be jailed if they returned home because they were considered draft dodgers.

I can remember watching the horror of the nightly news with my mother and brothers. Walter Cronkite was a well-known news anchorman that was broadcasting the nightly news. I can still remember hearing his hoarse voice narrating the mistreatment of our fellow human beings. Seeing these images on TV still haunt me even to this day. They are forever etched in my mind, especially the image of Negro men and women being tear-gassed, beaten, clubbed, and dragged through the streets by White police officers while others were being chased and bitten by their police dogs. There is also the brutal memory of several White firemen spraying the crowd of peaceful protesters with their powerful fire hoses. I always wondered to myself how many of those police officers and firemen that treated us this way were Christians? I asked God, "Does our lives matter too?"

My Sport Heroes and Early Church Life

I was so proud of the African American Olympic athletes Tommie Smith and John Carlos who stood on the winner's podium at the 8 Olympics with their gold and bronze medals proudly displayed around their necks. Tears came to my eyes the moment I realized that they were peacefully protesting to the world, just like what Martin Luther King Jr. wanted us to do. They had their heads bowed down and their black gloved fist were raised in the air, signaling to the world stage that racial discrimination and violence against our people was alive and happening in the United States, a land that claimed to be the land of the free and the home of the brave. Later that night, they were both suspended and ordered to leave the Olympic village within forty-eight hours for just silently protesting. They both became heroes in our community.

It seems like sports was the only way that we could get the recognition and the respect that we all deserved as a race. We had great sports heroes and champions such as the late Ernie Davis, who was the first Negro Heisman trophy winner in 1961; Cassius Clay, also known as Muhammad Ali, in boxing; Jim Brown in football; Hank Aaron in baseball; and Walt Chamberlain in basketball, to name a few. I cannot remember if we had any Negroes that played professional golf, tennis, hockey, or soccer at that time. One thing for sure, golf did have their share of professional, hopefully well- paid, Negro caddies.

My hometown of Plainfield had our own sports heroes that we wanted to be like too. There was Milt Campbell, who was the first African American athlete to win an Olympic gold medal in the decathlon in the 1964 Olympics. He later played in the NFL for the

25

Cleveland Browns. I met him because I was a friend and classmate of his son, Milt Campbell Jr. I played over their house too. Milt Campbell Jr. and I played on the same high school football freshmen team and ran track together. Vic Washington was another professional football player from Plainfield that played in the NFL for the San Francisco 49ers. And there was Rod Plummer who was from my neighborhood and who I personally knew. His four younger brothers were my friends. He was the first Black to play quarterback for Princeton University (1969–1971) and the first Black quarterback to play for an Ivy League school. Rod once led the nation in passing yardage. I tried to listen to all Princeton's home games on the radio. I was proud to hear the radio announcer call out his name during the games, especially when he said Rod Plummer from Plainfield, New Jersey. My dad was also a surprisingly good softball player as well. I used to love watching him play for the Twenty Plus club. My dad was one of my sports heroes too.

Kevin Bowe, who was a friend from our neighborhood, was one year older than me. We played sandlot football and baseball with him. He spent time together with us at my house and at the Woodland/Maxson School playground. Kevin was big and strong, muscles everywhere, but one of the nicest guys you would ever meet. On top of being a star athlete, Kevin was smart too. He made the honor roll every year in school since junior high school and was the class of 1975 salutatorian. Kevin had the greatest potential and skills to be that one kid in our neighborhood destined to fulfill our childhood dreams of becoming a professional athlete. Kevin was the captain of our high school football and made the New Jersey all- state football team during his junior and senior year in high school as a middle linebacker. He earned a full scholarship to the University of Virginia where he was a feared defensive end.

26

We also had another friend named Ben Nokey Johnson. He lived close by our neighborhood. We played against his neighborhood team from Seidler field in sandlot football and baseball. We also played against him in Little League baseball. Nokey was a star basketball player and captain of our high school team. He made to the 1975 Courier News All-star high school basketball team. Everyone who knew Nokey was optimistic that he would play professional basketball. He was in the same 1975 Plainfield High School graduating class with Kevin Bowe. We all were proud when he got a full basketball scholarship to Fairleigh Dickinson University, where he was a star freshman point guard. It was a sad day not only for all of Plainfield, but for college sports, in January 1976 when we got the news that Ben Nokey Johnson was killed in an automobile accident after returning from his college basketball game. Nokey was only eighteen years old when he died.

Mr. Warren Henry, our Tuskegee airman neighbor, was also a Plainfield high school football star. He played fullback and sometimes played quarterback for Plainfield High School (1938). The record did not say that he was the starting quarterback; however, this would still make him the first Negro playing quarterback for Plainfield High School. We must realize this was 1938.

Recently, I was blessed to read a newspaper article from 1938. It said,

> Plainfield High School beat our rival Westfield High School largely due to the brilliant running of the team's Negro backfield duo of hard-hitting Warren Henry and fancy-foot stepping Chris Lipscombe.

It was interesting that the article made sure that the readers knew that they were both Negro players. The article went on to say that Warren Henry played a great game. He scored a touchdown and played on defense too and had an interception. I was also given a copy of the team's 1938 photo that showed Chris Lipscombe and Warren Henry as the only two Negro players on their team.

Plainfield HS football 1938. Warren Henry no. 25 and Chris Lipscombe no. 27

This meant that they had to be exceptionally good to play on this team. There were no Negro players in the NFL, nor was there a Negro Football league in 1938 until after World War II. Very few Negroes were allowed to play college football during that time. I bet they both would have been great in college football and would had played professional football if Negros would have had the opportunity to play back then. Mr. Henry is a legend in my book. He deserves the recognition of being a Tuskegee Airmen and a high school football star. Later in life, Mr. Henry worked with youth in New York and New Jersey. He retired as a high school guidance counselor. Mr. Henry was a mentor and all-around hero in our community as well as in New York. My hero Mr. Henry died on October 22, 1991.

Growing up in New Jersey, you had to be either a New York Yankees fan or a New York Mets fan. I became a Yankee fan because I loved Babe Ruth, who was my baseball idol. Yankee Stadium was known as the "House That Babe Ruth Built." The Babe, who also was called the Great Bambino, was the all-time home run king with 714 home runs. My father would take us to Yankee Stadium to see the Yankees play and to Shea Stadium to see the Mets play. It was exciting to hear the roar of the crowd whenever someone hit a home run, stole a base, or there was a double play. Eating hot dogs with that Gulden mustard slapped on these hot dogs was one of the reasons we were so excited to go to the stadium and watch the games. I would eat as many hot dogs that my father would allow.

The next year, in 1969, the "Amazing Miracle" Mets won the World Series. They had a lot of talented players on their championship team. Four of these players were Negro players like Cleon Jones, Tommy Agee, Don Clendenon, and Ed Charles. Tommy Agee was my favorite player on the Mets team.

For a Black kid, playing professional sports and being a good athlete like our sports heroes sounded like a clever way to get paid and get out of Plainfield. Playing professional baseball or football on a championship team was a pipe dream for all of us kids growing up in my neighborhood. We played a lot of sandlot baseball, and we played tackle football against other neighborhood teams to sharpen our skills so that one day we too could play college sports and someday make it to the pros. My brothers and I played little league baseball for the same team, the Indians. They were both older than me. Sammy was twelve, and Isaac was eleven, so they played on the major league Indians. I was nine at this time, so I played on the minor league Indians.

All three of us turned out to be good baseball players. Isaac and Sammy both made the 1967 and 1968 Little

29

League all-star team. They were coached by Plainfield's own legendary Little League baseball coach named Mr. Gatti. He was a short man with a deep voice. His mannerisms and looks reminded you of Yogi Berra, the legendary New York Yankees baseball coach. One thing that was for certain, Mr. Gatti loved and enjoyed coaching young kids on the fundamentals of baseball. He coached the Indians into the 1968 Little League World Series.

That summer my mother and father were experiencing some kind of marital difficulties. One day when we returned home from our baseball practice, Mom was standing in the door crying. She had our suitcases packed.

My aunt Betty Morris was parked in the driveway with the engine running, waiting in the car to take us to the airport. Mom explained to us that we had to leave right away before Dad got home from work. We were all going to Columbus, Ohio, except for our dad. Mom said that we were going to visit her brother, our uncle Jake Mitchell, for a little while. Mom was mad with our father, so she decided to leave and take a break from him for a while. Boy! The timing could not have been worse. We were really upset that we had to leave two days before the start of the baseball Little League championship game. We all started crying when we realized that this meant that my brothers would miss playing in the game. This also meant that I would miss watching my brothers playing in the championship game too. That also meant that I would not be there either because I was also one of their batboys too when I was not playing for the minor league Indians.

The Indians were the east end champions that had to play the west end champions, the Pirates. Whichever team won the one-game series would be crowned the champion. My brothers both made the Little League all-stars team. Sammy was the league's batting champion with a batting average of .473. I could not help but think that the Indians had their two best players not playing with

30

them. There was no way that the Indians could win without their two best players and most importantly me as their batboy.

We eventually returned home a couple of weeks later. It was heartbreaking when we found out that the Indians lost. The Indians lost the championship game to the west end league champions, Pirates, 5–2. We were mad as heck with Mom for a little while because we knew that had my brothers and I been there and played, the Indians would have easily won the championship game.

The next two years I played first base for the major league Indians. I was a good baseball player.

I made the Little League all-star teams both years. On my last year with the Indians, at age twelve, we made it to the Little League championship game, but we lost it to a close game with the same Pirates, 3–2. I was the league's runner-up to the most valuable player, or MVP, award. My teammate Mark Witcombe, who was White and our star pitcher, had two more votes than I did and was chosen as the MVP. Mark and I, along with my neighborhood friend Butch Gray, made the tri-county all-star team that played the best teams outside Plainfield.

I also played running back for the Plainfield Blue Angels Pop Warner football team when I was nine until age twelve. I was a good running back. I ran a couple of touchdowns from the line of scrimmage and gained a lot of yardages when I was handed the ball. My father was in the stands when I ran a sixty-yard kickoff return for a touchdown. I can still remember seeing him in the corner of my eyes while I was running the touchdown. I heard him shouting and bragging to everyone around him, "That's my boy!"

My freshman year in high school I was on the football, wrestling, and track team. I can safely say that I was famous because I was the first Black pole vaulter for our school. My highest vault was fourteen feet. I was proud to play on several different teams for the Plainfield High School

Cardinals. I was okay but not good enough to play college football. It did not matter anyway because I knew I was destined for the Army.

When it came down to attending church, my family was like most Negro families in the sixties. We had several Christian denominations to choose from. You were either Baptist, Church in God in Christ, Holiness, or Methodist. My mother was the Methodist in our family. My father chose to attend the Lutheran church. I used to joke that we were Method-Lutherdist. Since Dad attended the Lutheran church, this meant that his boys, meaning my brothers Sammy, Isaac, and me, had to attend the Messiah Lutheran Church with him. I was the youngest of his three boys. Being that I was the youngest, I was more curious about God and the Holy Spirit, and I wanted to know more about Jesus than my brothers did.

We were the only Negro family that attended this Lutheran church. We enjoyed attending Sunday school at the church. We always had a snack break before we went into the sanctuary to sit with Dad for the morning service. The choir would sing some songs, and Pastor Dodge would preach his sermon. I never could understand what he was talking about, probably because I was too young. It was interesting but an alarming fact that the church was considered the most segregated place in America in 1969. But here we were, attending this mostly White church with no problems whatsoever. We were treated well, and no one appeared bothered that we were there. My sisters Yvonne, Linda, and Valerie were younger than me. They had to attend the African Methodist Episcopal (AME) Church with our mother. By now we all had accepted Jesus Christ as our Savior. Later that year, Dad had all six of us kids baptized at the Messiah Lutheran Church by Pastor Dodge. There was no doubt in my mind that Dad did love Jesus and he was saved by grace, but I also believe that my father's motivation for us attending the Messiah

32

Lutheran Church was strictly a business decision. Many of his customers were parishioners at this church. Dad owned a floor waxing, house cleaning, and window washing business. He was so proud of being a successful Negro businessman. He named his company Sam and Sons after himself, and he claimed that we were part-owners too. My father was a good provider and a good dad. Dad worked two jobs to make sure that we had everything that we needed. Even though Dad had his own business, he also worked a full-time job in the evening, at a company called Koppers Coal. It produced black tar that was used to pave driveways and streets. Dad worked there for the medical and life insurance and for the retirement benefits. These same benefits would have been too costly for him to afford as a small-business Negro businessman.

Life in the Seventies and a Look Back into the Sixties

By the early 1970s, the Temptations had a hit song called "A Ball of Confusion." Talking about a ball of confusion, hell, I did not know back then if I was a Negro, African American, Black, or a colored person. One thing that I knew for certain was that there were people that wanted to hurt us, degrade us or wanted to keep us riding on the back of the bus, and called us boys using the N- word. I was called all those things before including many other slangs not worth repeating today. I soon discovered, to my amazement, when I saw my original 1958 New Jersey–issued birth certificate for the first time, that my race was strangely recorded as "Colored." It was interesting to see that my parents' race were listed on my certificate as Negroes. My brothers' birth certificates listed their race as Negroes as well. I used to brag and joke with my two older brothers that I was a colored boy while they were Negroes.

Wow!

I think by the early seventies, we had accepted with dignity the fact that we no longer wanted to be called Negro as a race because of the misuse and abuse of the word *Negro*. It was used as a derogatory word. Most of us preferred to be called something else, like Black or African Americans. I can remember singing to myself in my bedroom that I shared with my two brothers the song sung by James Brown, which was our slogan of the day. After the song was over, I would stand up with pride and shout the slogan out loud in my room two times, "Say it loud, I'm Black and I'm proud! Say it loud, I'm Black and I'm proud!" I was also motivated by a famous quote by Arthur Fletcher, who was the president of the United Negro College

Fund. He said, "A mind was a terrible thing to waste." This quote challenged me as a Black kid to study hard and learn as much as I could so that I could be someone important in this world. I would always say to myself when I was studying, "The mind is a terrible thing to waste. I am Black, and I am proud."

In the seventies, life got a little better for our people. I would often look back to the sixties and think about how far we have come. My mind was shaped in the sixties, by watching shows and movies on the television, like *The Wizard of Oz*, *To Kill a Mockingbird*, and the *Incredible Shrinking Man*. These were my favorite movies that I loved watching while I was growing up. Only one of the three movies had a Negro main character. It was in the movie *To Kill a Mockingbird*. His real name was Brock Peters, and he played the role of the alleged criminal Tom Robinson, a humble, innocent stereotypical-looking dark-skinned Negro man. He had a wife and three small children in this movie. He was on trial in a small Alabama town for the rape of a White woman that he said he never committed.

This was an emotional movie for me because I thought that this was a real-life story with real people playing their parts. This movie was my introduction to racial injustice and prejudice against our people by the court system and some White people. The theme of the movie was good versus evil. Tom Robinson was easily convicted by an all-White jury of twelve men. He was later shot and killed at the end of the movie. They said Tom tried to escape while being transported to prison. I was sad when the movie ended because I really thought that Tom Robinson was a real person that was falsely convicted by this jury of White men. I really thought that he died for nothing.

My favorite shows and cartoons back in the sixties were Tennessee Tuxedo, Bozo the Clown, Superman, Popeye the Sailor Man, Captain Kangaroo, and Mister Roger's Neighborhood. It was sad because I cannot remember seeing any kids that looked like me or an adult Negro person in any of these shows. We did however have one Negro Hollywood star, and he was the first Negro to win an Academy Award for his role in the movie *Lilly of the Fields*. Sidney Poitier played in a lot of movies that were perfect for him, especially because he was a handsome and dark-skinned Negro. Other movies that he played in were *A Raisin in the Sun, Guess Who's Coming to Dinner*, and many other movies.

By the mid-seventies, we started having Black shows on television with real Black actors and not White actors playing Black men, like those on the *Amos 'n' Andy* show, which had two White guys with Black faces. It was making fun of us, mocking, and negatively stereotyping Negro people. Sitcoms like *Good Times, Sanford and Son*, and the *Jefferson's* were new shows that was funny back then; but they did not portray Blacks in a good light.

In the year 1970, we started to have Black movies with crazy- sounding titles like *Cotton Comes to Harlem*, which starred Black actors like Godfrey Cambridge and had a Black director named Ossie Davis. Soon, other Black movies with Black stars and Black directors started coming out as well, movies like the *Water-Melon Man, Shaft and Super Fly*, just to name a few. I asked myself why in the world someone would want to be called a nasty fly, super or not. We were simply happy to finally see Black movies and shows with Black stars or real people who looked like us on TV shows and in the movie theaters.

The early 1970s were a turbulent time for my family. My father would spend time in the nearby town of Westfield. That is where he did most of his cleaning business and where he would spend time with his friends and drink with them as well. Dad was a strong-willed man that did not mind flexing his muscles and money whenever he spent time in Westfield. Dad was popular in the small Black neighborhood of Westfield call Khaki Ola. Dad would hire people from this neighborhood. Dad was proud of himself, and he had a good heart. He would lend money to people that he knew and trusted when they needed it the most. Everyone that borrowed money from Dad were good at paying him back on time. They nicknamed him Uncle Sam because his name was Sam. He had lots of money, and he was good to everyone in this community. Dad was like most Black men in his day, or should I say, from the Jim Crow South. He did not have a high school education growing up in Kingsland, Georgia, but he did have street smarts and business sense.

My father was also well-known and liked by most of the police officers on the Westfield Police Department. Dad said there were a few police officers that disliked him for being an N-word with money. He was also someone who they could easily set up and arrest for drinking and driving and for driving without license. Dad did drink beer a lot, and liquor sometimes too, but I never saw him drinking to the point where he was impaired to drive. Dad only drank on the weekends, only because Mom would not allow him to drink on weekdays. Dad was a social drinker and was also smart enough to know better when he could not drive. My father claimed that he was falsely accused. He did admit to my mother when she bailed him out of jail that he did drink a few beers that night, but he swore to Mom that he was not drunk when he was arrested. What was a Black man going to do to dispute these charges in those days? To be honest, Dad made himself an easy target to be arrested by the police officers. He also knew better not to drive with suspended license.

Dad spent two months at two separate times in the Union County jail during a five-year period for his drinking and driving behaviors. Mom, along with us boys, had to keep his cleaning business going during those times he was in jail. We struggled financially at times when Dad was away. Mom had to pay his court fines first before buying food so that Dad could get out of jail earlier or when his time was up. This hurt us the most. Mom was a proud and strong Negro woman that really did not want to apply for food stamps or ask for handouts. Eventually, she had no choice but to get food stamps so that we could eat a regular meal. Our aunt Carrie and uncle Bernard would also travel from Manhattan, New York, to bring us government cheese, canned hams, peanut butter, and bags of potatoes. This helped when there was not enough money or food stamps to go around. Mom worked magic with the ham and cheese. We had ham this and cheese that. She also made the best potato soup in the world. We were also blessed by our neighborhood butcher who would set aside the end pieces of slice lunch meat that he would give to Mom for a small price.

Mom had to make us thick and sometimes lumpy sandwiches with the lunch meat because of the way they were cut. We did not care because they tasted good. Mom would also say that this meat was thick so that it could stick to our stomachs. Boy, was she right! We were simply happy to have something good to eat. Mom made sure none of us went to bed hungry.

Pastor Dodge, the pastor of Messiah Lutheran Church, was a godsend to my family. He would visit us every week and was extremely helpful to our family during these times of crises. Pastor Dodge and the church made sure that we had food, clothing, and spiritual guidance. He also made sure that we attended Sunday school every Sunday, church, and Vacation Bible School during the summer months. My favorite three songs that we would sing in church and Bible school were "Jesus Loves Me This I Know," "Go Tell It on the Mountain," and "This Little Light of Mine." Our family was well like by the church members. One summer they sent me and my brothers to a weeklong church summer camp. We were the only Black kids that were at the camp. Everyone treated us the same. We had a fun time at the camp. It was strange at the time because everyone there kept calling us Brother

Sammy, Brother Isaac, and me as Brother Lloyd as if "Brother" was our first name. The church and camp activities taught me a lot about God, Jesus, and the Holy Ghost. I loved Pastor Dodge and the church for sending us to this camp and what they did overall to help our family while Dad was serving his time.

My interest in God and the seeds of helping other families that had similar crisis led me to the idea that I could do something to help others too. My journey and my desires to be an ambassador in training for Christ started growing more especially when Dad was not around. My mother and several of her Christian friends would hold prayer meetings every weekend in our basement and sometimes across the street over at our neighbor Ms. Parker's house. Mother Tanner was a gifted and spirit-filled elderly Black lady who was in her sixties. She would lead these meetings. I would sneak on the top of the basement steps and listen in on their meetings. I was amazed by the way that they were worshipping God.

One of these occasions, when I was twelve, I got my first encounter with the Holy Ghost. I fell back on the top steps, bumped the back of my head, and started speaking in tongues. After a while, they knew I was there. Mom came up to the top of the steps, prayed for me, and explained to me what had just happened. They did not mind that I stayed on the top of the steps as long as I was quiet. We also had a next-door neighbor named Pastor Curtis Burton. He was a Holiness pastor that was always praying and speaking in tongues. He was so loud that I could hear him praying from inside his house while I slowly walked by on the sidewalk. There were times that I stopped to listen to what he was praying about. I felt many times in my spirit that he was praying for me and speaking directly to me. I can still hear his deep voice and his spirit praying for me. I will always cherish these moments. Amen.

Dad returned home in 1975 after serving his second and final time in jail. We were all excited when he returned home. The excitement of him returning home only lasted less than one hour for me. I quickly learned that Dad lost his driver's license because of his arrest record and spending time in jail. Because I was the youngest of his three boys, that meant that I was volunteered by my mother and brothers to be Dad's designated driver, regardless of whether I wanted to drive or not. The only problem with driving Dad around was that he could not talk without yelling whenever I did something wrong like miss a turn that he would point to or tell me at the last minute to make a right or left turn.

To be honest, it was not all that bad because I got to use his car whenever I needed it. I felt important because I drove Dad's car to high school. I would also use his car to drive to church and would use his car to hang out with my best friend at the time, Howard Evans. Howard and I would drive all over Plainfield and Westfield. Just like any teenagers with a car, we would go hang out at the park, cruise the town, and hang out over girls' houses too. Dad was smart enough to know that eventually that I would get pulled over by the Westfield police because they knew the car that Dad drove. Dad had a lot of respect for the police. He knew in his heart that I would eventually get pulled over by them. He wanted to make sure that I was prepared for that day, so he taught me how to respect law enforcement and what to do as a young Black teen to be safe when they did pull me over.

Dad said, "Son if you are pulled over, please stay in the car. Get your driver's license and insurance card ready. Place both hands on the steering wheel. Be respectful, answer all questions by the officer and say 'No, sir' or 'Yes, sir.' You will do fine if you trust my words."

Dad was right. There were times that the Westfield police would pull me over several times hoping that I was Dad. They would be disappointed, but they were nice when they realized that I was Sam Glover's youngest son. They would always ask how my dad was doing. My response was, "He is doing well and staying out of trouble, Officer."

Dad liked to go out at night, especially on the weekends to hang out and drink at different bars and clubs. His favorite hangout spots were in his favorite town of Westfield. He loved going out to Tony's Tavern and the Centennial Lodge. I would drop him off at one of these places and pick him up later when he wanted to come back home. There were many times when I would get there on time to pick him up, then he would decide at the last minute that he was not ready to go. There were no cell phones then. I would wait in the car for an hour or so sitting outside in the parking lot for him to come out to the car. I was seventeen, a high school senior, and some of these evenings, it was cold sitting in this car with little heat. And if they were on weekday or Sunday nights, I had to go to school on the next day.

When Dad was inside these bars, I really did not mind waiting because I would listen to Christian programs on the AM radio. I was always excited around 10:00 p.m. because I knew that Reverend Ike was coming on the air. I had to fight through the static of the AM radio to hear him well. He was a famous Black pastor, preacher, evangelist, and author. His real name was Rev. Frederick J. Eikerenkoetter. I thought, that with a name like that, it was easy to understand why he called himself Reverend Ike. He would always sound so good to me, especially when he preached on prosperity, about the "Power of I Am," and about "Money Cometh." Listening to this kind of preaching was inspiring and laid the foundation of my early ministry. I had fun going into the bathroom mirror imitating his preaching style. I called myself Reverend Ike. Jr.

I started watching Pat Robertson and the *700 Club* on TV and programs featuring televangelists like Jimmy Swaggart, James Robison, T. L. Osborn, John Osteen, and

41

R. W. Schambach. I was told that Reverend Ike was on the TV; however, I never found out what channel or time that he was on. R. W. Schambach was my favored TV preacher, especially when he held those big-tent meetings and crusades. I tried to learn something from each of these men of God. I also had a love for gospel music. My favorite artists were James Cleveland, Shirley Caesar, James Moore, and the Williams Brothers. I believe that the events of the 1960s and early '70s were the catalyst that began my thinking more about God, life, death, race, career, and religion.

Beginning of Army Life—God had a Rescue Plan

It was April 1975, and the Vietnam War was ending. By September of that year, I started my senior year of high school. It has always been my plan since I was a kid playing army with Brian and my other friends that I was going to join the Army after graduation. I joined the New Jersey Army National Guards as a weekend warrior with two of my high school classmates, David Barnett and Greg Goodwin. We were given Army uniforms and attended weekend drills at our Westfield Army National Guard Armory while we were still in high school. We did get paid to attend these drills. We graduated from high school on June 17, 1976. By July 11 or should I say twenty-five days later after we graduated, we left together to attend eight weeks of Army basic training at Fort Dix, New Jersey. We got lucky, and we were assigned to the same basic training unit. It was funny when we all had to get all our hair cut off. There were young men from all over the United States that were in our basic training unit.

Our drill sergeants on the first day were the meanest people that you could ever meet. All they wanted to do on the first day was to yell, cuss, and call us names that were not pretty. They would also make us all do push-ups whenever someone from our unit messed something up.

Basic training was hard and challenging. We would volunteer to attend weekly church services together to get out of doing extra duty. Eight weeks later, we graduated from basic training. Dave Barnett and I went to Fort Jackson, South Carolina, to attend clerk typist school, while Greg Goodwin went on to Fort Eustis, Virginia, to become a helicopter mechanic.

I liked being at Fort Jackson. I would attend the post-church services and volunteer to help around the church there.

One day, when I was pulling hall monitor duties in our barrack, Dave Burnett came to me with tears in his eyes. He told me the sad news that Kevin Bowe, our friend who played college football for the University of Virginia and who had the aspirations of playing professional football, was killed while visiting his grandparents in Washington, DC. We were both devastated by the news. Kevin was our second friend within nine months that was tragically killed. Our other high school friend who played college basketball, also with professional aspiration, Ben Nokey Johnson, died in an automobile accident nine months earlier in January.

We all graduated from our training schools, and we returned to Plainfield. A week later I joined the regular Army because I wanted to get away and see the world. Being a clerk typist didn't seem macho enough for a young, gung ho soldier like me. I wanted to join the airborne infantry this time around. The Army career counselor tricked me into accepting a different combat job as a Nike Hercules missile crewmen. He looked at my test scores and said that I was a smart guy and that I could receive this training on the job (OJT). He also told me that I could get a better-paying job with an aerospace company than I would have as an infantry soldier once I complete my four-year agreement with the Army. So, I took it.

On January 11, 1977, I was sent to Germany as a young eighteen-year-old Army private E-2. I was assigned to a Nike Hercules nuclear missile site as a Nike Hercules missile crewman. The missile site was isolated and in the middle of nowhere in a small German farming town called Schönborn. We were located twenty-five miles north of Kaiserslautern, which had a large Army and Air Force presence. The attitude of most of the soldiers that were stationed at this site was bad because of the isolation of being on a nuclear missile site. There were no women assigned to this site. To make matters even worse, there were a few remaining Vietnam-era draftees that were assigned at this site that did not want to be here or even in the Army for that matter. They made it a point to make sure everyone there knew it too. They were like poison to the morale of this unit and especially to the newly assigned young soldiers like me.

My second day there, I met my section sergeant. He did not like the idea that I did not go to school to be trained on the Nike Hercules missile system. He was not happy nor was he interested in training me either. So, he assigned me to the mess hall as a KP, meaning I washed dishes and pulled a lot of guard duty for my first six months. There was no one there that was interested in training me on the missile system or helping me on anything. The hardest part of being there was that there was no one there that was interested in talking about God with me either. We did have an Army chaplain assigned to our unit, but he was of no spiritual help to me. It seems like he had his own problems too. He must have been assigned for moral support only. I cannot ever recall if he conducted any church services or Bible studies. Smoking cigarettes and hashish was a common habit for everyone there except a few of us. Beer, rum, Jim Beam with Coca-Cola, and brass monkey with ice cubes were everyone's drinks of choice. I wasn't a saint, so that included me too.

I quickly fell into a dark hole and a life of sin. I became a lonely, angry, and a suicidal young soldier. My childhood dream of being a good soldier was slowly drifting away. I thought seriously about quitting the Army a couple of times but quickly changed my mind because I did not want to be known as a quitter, nor did I want to embarrass my family and return home to Plainfield with a bad conduct or dishonorable discharge. I was so disappointed about my life that I did not write or call home to let my mother know where I was stationed at in the world. Mom eventually had to call the American Red Cross to know if I was still alive or not. My commander informed me that the American Red Cross called him. He directed me to call

45

home right away. I did call home the same day. I was happy when Momma answered the phone. I can still hear her broken voice, and I can still sense the tears in Momma's eyes when she heard my voice and realized that her baby boy was still alive. This was the first time that we spoke since I arrived in Germany. I lied to her and told her that things were good. I did apologize to my mother for not calling home and for not letting her know where I was stationed at in Germany. Momma forgave me, and she prayed for me before she hung up the phone. I was so angry and disappointed about my life and the terrible fact that this was the first time that I truly lied to my mother. My mother has always been a good mother, and she certainly deserved better.

Things got so bad for me at one point during my first six months in Germany that I came awfully close to committing suicide while pulling guard duty one night in a twenty-foot-high guard tower. I was alone in the tower, and I had a loaded M16 rifle with a round in the chamber pointed at my head. Tears were clouding my eyes. At the moment when I tried to pull the trigger, my right arm down to my trigger finger went numb. I could not pull the trigger, nor could I see the trigger because of all those tears that were now flowing from my eyes. Suddenly, I could hear the praying voice of my mother clearly as if she were next to me in the guard tower. She was calling my name and pleading the blood of Jesus over my life. I could feel her warm presence, and I could smell the perfume that she loved wearing all the time inside the guard tower. It was overwhelming. It could only had been God that allowed me to hear her praying and sense her presence at that precise moment in time. I could also feel the warmth of a spirit that forcefully yelled at me, "*Stop, we have need of you!*" I felt in my spirit that this was not God, but my guardian angel. I stopped as he instructed me to do so. I wiped away my tears and looked around to see what the spirit looked like. He was gone by then. Prior to this event, I was angry with God, and I blamed Him for sending me here. I totally forgot about my ministry and seldom did I think about God during this empty time in my life.

I was ashamed for what I was trying to do. I quickly fell to my knees, and I asked God to forgive me. I felt his grace and mercy. I knew in my heart, and I felt it in my soul that He did forgive me. I thought about Psalm 30:5, which says, "Weeping may last through the night, but joy comes in the morning." And I could remember the words that my mother said to me the day that I left for the Army. Mom said, "Always remember this about the Lord— 'For the Lord, your God goes with you; he will never leave you or forsake you.'"

The following week my old section sergeant left, and my joy came by his replacement, Staff Sergeant Dave Brookshire. He was a godsend and a part of God's rescue plan to save my life and to put me back on the right path of life. Staff Sergeant Brookshire quickly pull me out of the mess hall, away from pulling all that guard duty, and away from a life of destruction and out of that miry clay (Ps. 40:1–3). He started having other soldiers training me on the missile system and the job that I was tricked into taking by that Army guidance counselor. The one thing that the Army guidance counselor got right was when he said that I was a smart guy and that I could learn this job by on-the-job training. He had that part right. It did not take long for me to learn the job. I soon became a motivated soldier and one of the best soldiers on-site.

Life on the Rebound

Despite the internal struggles that I had during my first six months in Germany, I was grateful to God for given me a new song and a U-turn in life and to Staff Sergeant Brookshire for giving me a second chance to prove to myself that I was a good soldier. I wanted to give God and Staff Sergeant Brookshire the reassurance that I was not a waste of their time. I soon became one of the best soldiers there. Every year I would get selected as part of a team of our best soldiers to fly to the Crete Islands of Greece to take part in our annual service practice. This was a live fire evaluation of our unit to figure out our combat readiness and our effectiveness. Our assignment was to build a Nike Hercules missile from the ground up and fire it out to the sea at an imaginary aircraft where it would explode in the air. My last year doing this exercise, I was the fire panel operator that operated the missile controls that fired this Nike Hercules missile. I was proud of myself when the signal was given to me to launch the missile. I can still hear the command and countdown signal dancing in my head for me to fire this missile,
Ten...nine...eight...seven...six...five...four...three...two...one...fire! And the feeling of me operating the toggle switch that caused the ground to shake with the thunderous roar of the Nike Hercules missile as it took off into the sky that overlooked the Mediterranean Sea.

Nike Hercules missile, Crete Island, Greece, 1978

I came as an Army private E-2. Within two years, despite my first six months of difficulties, I got promoted to sergeant E-5. It has always been at the back of my mind that I was following 1 Corinthians 10:31, which says, "Whatever you do, do all to the glory of God," nor did I realize that God was with me the whole time, according to Hebrews 13:5, which says, "I will never leave you, nor forsake you," and according to Philippians 4:13, which says, "I can do all things through Christ who strengthen me." Amen.

Being in Germany was not all about being a soldier. There was a nearby German town called Rockenhausen that had a disco and some nice German restaurants. There was one German restaurant that had the best pizza I had ever eaten. The disco was the hanging spot to dance and meet German women. There was also Sembach Air Base and Ramstein Air Base that many of us love going to hang out and party with American military women. I had a 1968 Volkswagen beetle sedan that I drove all around Germany with my friends. My nickname was Star Child because I had a light-blue baseball cap with a silver star in the middle of this hat.

It was in January 1979, with a year still left on my three-year assignment to Germany, when the miraculous happened. I got unexpected orders assigning me to Fort Bliss, Texas, with a reporting date of April 1, 1979. This surprise reassignment allowed me to leave Germany nine months earlier than expected.

As soon as I got to Fort Bliss, I quickly reestablished my relationship with God. I started attending the church services on the base, and I found myself reading my Bible and studying Christian literature every chance I got. I got blown away when I read 2 Corinthians 5:17–21.

> Therefore, if anyone *is* in Christ, *he is* a new creation; old things have passed away; behold, all things have become new. Now all things *are* of God, who has reconciled us to Himself through Jesus Christ, and has given us the ministry of reconciliation, that is, that God was in Christ reconciling the world to Himself, not imputing their trespasses to them, and has committed to us the word of reconciliation. Now then, we are ambassadors for Christ, as though God were pleading through us: we implore *you* on Christ's behalf, be reconciled to God. For He made Him who knew no sin to be sin for us, that we might become the righteousness of God in Him.

I also read Philippians 4:13, which says, "I can do all things through Christ who strengthens me." Amen.

I felt forgiven again and motivated after reading these verses. This rekindled the fire in me. I realized that I had a purpose in life as an ambassador for Christ and as a Christian soldier in the Army. I knew then that God had a need for me to do something for his kingdom. At this point, I was not sure what it was. I started spending hours reading the Bible, praying, and gathering up information about being a minister. I wanted to prepare myself for what God had in store for me. I attended the post-church service where I was able to assist the chaplain doing work around the chapel. He took an interest in my goals of one day being a minister. The chaplain provided me with information about schools to attend and other helpful information about the process to becoming an Army chaplain.

It was January 1980 when I received orders to become an Army recruiter. I then went to recruiting school at Ft. Benjamin Harrison, Indiana. I was the top graduate in my class. This allowed me to pick my assignment to where I could go. I could have picked any major city in the United States including Hawaii. I choose Cleveland, Ohio. Why? I do not know.

In April 1980, I received my orders and was assigned to Cleveland, Ohio. I quickly joined the New Life Independent Fellowship Ministerial Church, which was a small nondenominational church in Cleveland, where I was later licensed as a minister. A year later I met and quickly fell in love with a beautiful young lady named Tammy Bland. Monies were tight. We dated for a year before I asked her to marry me. Tammy said yes. I was an incredibly happy man knowing that I was marrying the love of my life. Tammy wanted to have a big wedding, but her family did not have the money to pay for the wedding. Having a big wedding was not that important to me. So, on July 30, 1982, we went to the justice of peace and got married. I wore my Army dress blue uniform, and Tammy wore a beautiful white dress with a red sweater. We did not have any witnesses except for God.

Our wedding day photo

I was an extraordinarily successful recruiter in Cleveland. I was mentored by three successful recruiters. Staff Sergeant Elijah Mitchell, Sergeant Charles Jones, and Sergeant Vance O. Hunter took me under their wings and taught me the ropes of recruiting. I was one of the top recruiters in the Cleveland recruiting district. I received many recruiting awards for being the top recruiter for several different months. After three years of successful recruiting, I earned next to the highest recruiting award that you earn as an Army recruiter, which is the gold recruiters' badge with three sapphires. I was proud of my accomplishment, and I was proud of all the young people that I recruited for the Army. Upon completing my recruiting assignment, I left Cleveland as an extraordinarily successful Army recruiter and a happily married man with a child on the way.

My next assignment took me back to Fort Bliss, Texas, from 1983 until 1986. I was sent back to Fort Bliss to train on a newly developed, advanced Patriot missile system, which was designed to shoot down advanced jet fighters. I completed my training. I was assigned to HHB 2/43rd Air Defense Artillery battalion at Fort Bliss as a newly promoted staff sergeant E-6. We were the second Patriot missile battalion formed in the United States Army. I was given an assignment as the section sergeant in charge of the section that was called missile reload. I had great soldiers assigned to me, like Sergeants Eddie Royal, Sam Adams, Carl Brown and Specialist Dana West, Eric Miller, Larry Graham. I had one tough female specialist Tawana Hill that was assigned to my section. Our assignment was to create procedures to reload four Patriot missiles onto the launchers after the missiles were fired. The vehicle that we started with to conduct the missile reload was a wrecker-type truck that looked more like a big tow truck. This vehicle was slow and cumbersome that made the reload process slow. We had to reload the missiles on to a flatbed truck trailer.

This meant that we had to have two vehicles to do the reload at first. Finally, the Army provided us with a new vehicle, which replaced the wrecker truck, called a HEMTT wrecker (short for heavy expanded mobility tactical truck). The truck had its own crane at the back end of the truck. This allowed us to reload the missiles onto our one truck instead of using a wrecker truck and trailer. This made reloading much quicker. It took us a little time to develop these procedures and to get them right. The procedures that we created are the same procedures used thirty years today by all Patriot missile units around the world. My team was proud of our accomplishments. Tammy and I both loved Jesus. We attended the church services together on base at Fort Bliss chapel. There were times that we would also visit local churches in the El Paso area to attend revivals as well. Even though I was a licensed minister, I could not minister on the base chapels because I was not a seminary-trained chaplain.

By this time, Tammy and I had three children, born within a three-year period. All three of our children were born at Fort Bliss's William Beaumont army hospital. Tammy and I used to boast that we were just doing what God asked us to do according to Genesis 1:28 where God said that we must be fruitful, multiply, and replenish the earth. I felt that God had to be pleased with me and Tammy. God blessed us with three beautiful gifts.

Tiesha was our first gift. She was a baby girl born on February 15, 1984. Our second gift was a son, who was born ten months later on December 24. His name, for a few minutes, at birth was Lloyd Calvin Glover Jr. But because he was born on Christmas Eve, I felt led by the Spirit to change his name to Christopher Emanuel in honor of our Savior. God promised me that I would someday have another son that I could name after me. Latasha was our third gift, a baby girl born on February 17, 1986. We were hoping for a boy, but God gave us a beautiful daughter instead. Being a man of faith, I knew in my spirit that God was going to bless us with a fourth child, who was going to be the baby boy that God had promised. I considered being a godly husband and a godly father as part of my early ministry.

Later that year, I was given orders reassigning me back to recruiting duty. This time I was assigned to my home state of New Jersey as an Army recruiting station commander, in charge of seven Army recruiters assigned to the Trenton Army recruiting station. I had four regular Army recruiters and three Army reserved recruiters assigned to my recruiting station. My family was allowed to live on the Fort Dix Army base. Things were not all roses for me during this period, 1985 to 1989. I was so busy being an Army recruiter that basically I put my ministry on hold and I did not attend church services the whole time that I was in New Jersey.

The pressure to recruit high numbers of applicants and the need to work long hours just about seven days per week led to many recruiters breaking recruiting regulations and doing illegal stuff that clearly violated Army recruiting policies. Depending on what recruiting area that you were assigned, you had to violate Army policies just to be successful, to make your monthly recruiting quotas.

As a Christian and as a minister, this was too much for me, and I wasn't going to allow my recruiters to do anything illegal that would violate Army policies or my Christian values. My command was not happy with my leadership because my recruiting station was barely making our monthly recruiting quotas. We did however have several months when we did exceed our monthly recruiting goals. My commander knew that in order to be successful as a recruiter, you had to bend the rules to recruit high numbers of recruits. Even though my commanders preached on ethics and recruiting with integrity, they were willing to turn a blind eye, knowing that some of our best recruiter was recruiting unqualified applicant for the Army. They did not care just as long as the recruiter did not get caught. Once caught, an internal investigation would occur. If found guilty, the recruiter and maybe the recruiting station commander would get punished and, many times, they both would get relieved of his or her recruiting duties.

My commanders knew by then that I was not willing to allow my recruiters to violate Army policies to advance the officers' and senior sergeants' army careers. God had a hedge of protection over my career and life. He rewarded my honesty. I eventually got promoted to sergeant first class. A couple of months later after my promotion, I was reassigned and replaced by one of my assigned recruiters, who was a close friend of mine that was willing to do the illegal things that I was unwilling to do. I was assigned to another recruiting station that was even worse when it came to recruiting violations. This time I was assigned as an Army recruiter. This was not a demotion but a disappointment and a positional change. I survived the temptations of violating Army policies or violating my Christian values to make my recruiting quotas. I recruited with integrity and did enough overall to be successful.

I lost my beloved sister Linda and my father during the years that I was stationed in New Jersey. My father and sister did not live perfect lives, but one thing that they had in common was that they both loved the Lord and they both were saved by God's grace and mercy when Jesus said it was finished at the cross at Calvary.

Soon after my father's death, May 1989, I got my orders assigning me to a Patriot missile battalion, this time to the Federal Republic of Germany. I was assigned to the Giessen Army Depot as the platoon sergeant over the battalion's operations control center. I was also serving at the same time as the acting first sergeant of our headquarters battery HHB 4/43 air defense artillery during my first three months until a new first sergeant arrived from the States.

As soon as I arrived at my new unit, the first thing that I did was to ask about church. I was happy and surprised to find out that there was one at this location. The first Sunday I attended the depot's nondenominational church service. I joined their congregation. The service was led by a fellow soldier, Staff Sergeant George Gadson. He was a Holy Ghost–filled Church of God in Christ minister. We later found out that we were assigned to the same air defense battalion. My wife and my children soon arrived in Germany to be with me. Being that I was a senior sergeant, I was given the opportunity to live in a beautiful German community.

The townhouse that we lived in was in a German farming community. We soon became friends with many of our German neighbors. They really took to liking Tammy and our kids. They would invite us over to their beer gardens to eat German food and drink German beer and sodas with them. Of course, I drank the German sodas. I spend most of my time when I was off work running miles on their farm trails and back

56

dirt roads. I would listen to my gospel music; talk with God; and practice preaching to the cows, chickens, sheep, and pigs as I ran by them. I bet after a while the cows, chickens, sheep and pigs would say to each other, "Here comes that Jesus man again." Running out in the open air became my private time space with God.

My family attended church with me as well. When the weather was bad and the snow prevented us from attending church or Bible studies, I would conduct the services in our house with my family. Staff Sergeant Gadson's and my family became good friends. Our kids really enjoyed playing together. Staff Sergeant Gadson soon became my spiritual mentor. Within a brief period, I was allowed to join as a minister. I did not think to bring my minister's credentials with me to Germany, so basically, I thought this was a Church in God in Christ church and that I had to start over again by re-announcing my calling into ministry. I was glad when the church ministers prayed, laid hands on me, and accepted me as one of their ministers. Pastor Gadson allowed me as his newest minister to conduct sermonettes to increase my ministerial skills. I later found out that the mother of the church was the only one that wasn't in agreement with my acceptance as a minister in this church. I never did find out why. I gave it to God. Tammy was happy at first about me becoming a minister again, but after several months, she became cold to the thought of being a minister's wife.

After being in Germany for six months, I was sent to Alpha Battery 4/43 ADA to become the platoon sergeant over the fire control platoon. Being that I was a sergeant in charge of soldiers, I had to stay updated and knowledgeable on current events and the situations around the world that could have an impact on the United States military being deployed to a troubled spot around the world, especially with us being in Germany and what was going on in Europe (with the Cold War still going on since 1948).

We were in Germany on November 9, 1989, when the Berlin Wall fell. This was a pivotal event in world history, which marked the fall of the Iron Curtain and the beginning of the series of events that started the fall of communism and the reunification of East and West Germany. Within a year's time, the Soviet Union was dissolved. We were happy because we thought that this would lead to a time of peace and safety for the entire world. We later found out, by August 1990, that we were wrong!

The Beginning of the Gulf War

On August 2, 1990, Iraq's Army invaded and occupied Kuwait. Little did I know that Iraq's invasion would affect my life five months later. On August 17, the United States and thirty-nine other nations formed a coalition against Iraq's invasion and annexation of Kuwait. This included eleven countries from the Arab world. Operations Desert Shield was ramping up. The United States troop levels peaked to 580,000 troops that was sent to Saudi Arabia in preparation for the war that Saddam Hussein said will be the "mother of all battles" because of Iraq's weapons of mass destruction. Every day there were soldiers from other units at the Giessen Army Depot that were leaving for Operations Desert Shield.

It seemed like every week we had to send some of our soldiers and equipment from our unit to other Patriot missile units that were already deployed to the front lines in Saudi Arabia as replacements for soldiers that had to leave Saudi Arabia for whatever their reasons were and to also replace equipment that was damaged or was no longer working properly. I was told by my platoon leader, Lieutenant Brenda Rivera, that I had to prepare and send one of my best fire control operators, Sergeant Malcolm Weston, to one of the units already deployed in Saudi Arabia.

When I got the word that we had to send him, it felt like a gut punch because, as his sergeant, I loved him (and all my soldiers and their families) like a father loves his kids. It was painful when I had to tell him that he was leaving our unit and his family was headed to Saudi Arabia without us. It felt like I was talking to a dead man walking when I informed Sergeant Weston that he was selected by our chain of command to be deployed within the next several hours. Sergeant Weston was married with a young son. Another one of my soldiers, Specialist Dennis Mims, stepped up and volunteered to take Sergeant Weston's place. Specialist Mims was a single soldier and a close friend of Sergeant Weston. He wanted his friend to remain with his family. This was an unselfish act by Specialist Mims.

I wasn't happy that I had to send either of these men, but I had no choice. One of them had to go. Our command agreed to send Specialist Mims instead. I had to make an inventory of Specialist Mims's property and lock up his equipment just like I had to do a year earlier for an AWOL soldier and then again for another young soldier that was killed in a training accident. It was my hope and prayer that when this war was over that Specialist Mims would return to our unit. We all liked him, and we wanted him to be safe. I have been Specialist Mims platoon sergeant for the past two years. We talked and laughed about many different subjects but never talked about God, and he never expressed his religious belief before. Yes, I was a minister, but I was limited on what I could discuss with my subordinates. Being that Specialist Mims was leaving; I asked him if we could pray together for his safety and his safe return. He accepted my offer, and we prayed. We hugged and said our goodbyes. I had another soldier help him carry his bags to the truck that took him and two other soldiers that were also leaving.

From August 1990 until January 18, 1991, my unit in Germany was waiting for the call to be a part of Operation Desert Shield. This was an incredibly stressful time for our unit and especially for our families that remained with us in Germany. We knew that if we had to deploy, our families would be left in Germany without us. Regardless of our personal or family's situation, we still had to prepare and be ready to deploy just in case our unit got the call to go to war. Crazy things were happening. Soldiers were turning themselves in to our military dispensaries and hospitals looking to get mental evaluations that would cause them to be hospitalized or listed as nondeployable so that they would not be sent to the war.

There were other soldiers that were desperately filling out paperwork at the last minute in an effort trying to be classified as a conscientious objector so that they did not have to go to war. All these attempts by these soldiers to avoid from going to war failed. I asked one of our young soldiers how he felt about going to war. He said that he, like many of his fellow soldiers, joined the all-volunteer Army to go to school and to travel the world. Going to war and dying wasn't part of their plans.

We had one incident that involved one of our senior sergeants, who was stressed out just like everyone else in our unit. One evening he was trying to go home for the day when he noticed that there was a crowd of German citizens that were blocking the entrance and exit gates preventing him and other soldiers from leaving and coming on to the depot. They were gathered outside, protesting our involvement in Desert Shield. They did not like it, and they didn't want Germany to get involved in the war either. It wasn't funny at first but became funny after we heard that this senior sergeant (who I will not name fully, let's just say Sergeant First Class W) tried to sneak out of the back exit gate by the depot's helicopter landing pad that was always unattended and closed.

The accident report said he left in a hurry, laughing and looking behind him because he thought he was about to leave the depot and the protesting crowd behind. He did not realize that the traffic arm was down in front of him. He drove his car straight through the traffic arm, resulting in damages to the traffic arm, which had to be replaced. Once we heard about it and when he returned to the unit the next day, we laughed so hard with him and at him for days. One soldier laughed so hard that he peed on himself. The truth was that we really needed the laugh at this stressful time. This same Sergeant First Class W, to his credit, later became one of our heroes during the war.

The reactions to the stress and the real possibilities of us going to the war in the Gulf had soldiers walking around

61

their units like zombies bumping into walls. The stress of going to war was not just a problem in my unit in Germany. I bet this was a widespread problem across the Army and a problem across all branches of the military. At least twice a week we would hear stories about soldiers that were scared enough to the point that they were purposely injuring themselves.

We had to prepare by undergoing many types of medical examinations. We were given all types of untested and experimental vaccines like anthrax and other medications with names like botulinum toxoid and others that were simply too hard to pronounce. We were told by our army command that these would protect us against the chemical attacks, germ warfare, and many other weapons of mass destruction that was believed that Iraq had. We also had to complete our wills and decide for the safety of our families. Some of our soldiers started sending their families back to the States right away. The worst part of this process occurred during a briefing conducted by an Army chaplain who was a full colonel. His assignment was to explain to us that 55 percent or more of the soldiers that are going to be deployed to the Gulf will be killed because of Iraq's weapons of mass destruction. The sergeant in me told me to do a quick scan of the auditorium. I calculated in my mind that this meant that a little more than half or 213 of our 426 soldiers in this auditorium were going to die.

It was frightening and hard to process what the chaplain had just said to us about the percentage that was predicted that would die. The auditorium got quiet, and everyone stopped doing whatever they were doing and immediately looked up to see what else the chaplain was going to say next. His words were sharp and straight to the point. This made me feel numb. My head started pounding, and I felt like I was spinning. I could feel the sweat that was covering my head. My first thought was (but I was not 100 percent sure) to blame it on the stress of the moment and all the vaccines and medications that I had to take. They were all making me feel sick this way.

My thoughts quickly shifted to my wife, Tammy, and our kids. By now Tammy was nine months pregnant with our fourth child, the promised son that God told me that I would have. My soon-to-be- born son, Lloyd Calvin Glover Jr., is due to be born sometime during February. I quickly realized then that I would not be home for his birth if we got the call to go to war. It was also troubling that Tammy would be living in a German community all alone with my three young kids ages four, four, and two. Being that I was a soldier, I could only think about the two worst-case scenarios: what would happen if Tammy went into labor in the middle of the night and what would happen to my three kids if she did.

The tears started slowly flowing from my eyes at this point. I was now hurting because I just realized that I could be breaking a promise that I made to Tammy when we first got married that I would be in the delivery room during the birth of all our children. I put my head down, trying to hide my face and feelings from the soldiers that were nearby. It was hard wiping away the tears before I noticed that I was not alone. There was other Army-hardened soldiers that were not crying but were trying to wipe away their tears too. I am sure the other soldiers were thinking about their family situations as well.

I started having flashbacks about all those war movies that I had watched growing up. Movies about World War II and the Korean War. It seemed like every one of these movies had a scene showing a soldier or a Marine writing a letter to his pregnant wife back home. A sentence from his letter would read, "Honey, I will be home soon." The next sentence would read, "I love you. I can't wait to see you and my new baby." None of the soldiers could ever finish writing their letters because of an incoming attack by the enemy. The scene would always end with him kissing, folding, and tucking the letter in his shirt pocket, grabbing his rifle, and then heading off to the battle. The next scene would show the soldier fighting gallantly against the enemy and then you could see him being shot and killed in action.

After the battle has been won or the enemy attack had been repelled, the body of those KIA (killed in action) had to be collected, accounted for, tagged, and placed in body bags. His captain would review the list of casualties and see the soldier's body on the ground among the war's dead. He reaches over his body and does the cross symbol with his right hand over the soldier's lifeless body. He then gently removes one of his dog tags from around his neck and places the other dog tag in the fallen soldier's mouth, reaches into the fallen soldier's pocket, and finds the unfinished letter. The captain, showing little emotion, moves on to the next fallen soldier. He is battle-hardened because he has done this several times before from earlier battles.

Later in the movie, his captain would be seen finishing the fallen soldier's letter. The captain would add his remarks to the letter, informing the soldier's wife that her husband was killed in action, fighting courageously against the enemy and how good a soldier he was. He would add a sentence on how he died as a hero and how proud the fallen soldier would have been so proud to see her and their newborn child. Because of these movies and knowing that Tammy was pregnant and I could be going off to war scared me. I knew this was going to be my fate and that I was going to die just like these fathers-to-be. The words of the chaplain started ringing in my ears about me being one of those 213 soldiers that were going to die. I prayed, prayed, and prayed again to God for the next several days that my unit would not deploy to the Gulf countries of Saudi Arabia, Kuwait, or Iraq.

Getting the Call to Deploy to the War

On January 17, 1991, the aerial war started with the bombing of Iraq by the coalition war planes. They flew 2,774 sorties, or bombing runs on the first day. This operation was no longer called Desert Shield. The code name was now Operation Desert Storm. Later that night, we had a battalion meeting with our commanders, informing us that our battalion would not be deployed to the Gulf because we had a Jewish battalion commander that they did not want to send to that region. We were also told that they had all the Patriot missile units that were needed in Saudi Arabia at this time. We were relieved and celebrated the fact that we were not going to the war yet. I thanked God for answering my prayers.

The next day, on January 18, Iraq fired eight Scud missiles at Israeli cities of Haifa and Tel Aviv, slightly injuring twelve citizens of Israel and damaging residential buildings. Later that night, as soon as we got home, we received the alert call from our command that we were deploying. I remember packing my war equipment and my remaining battle uniforms into my war-ready duffel bag. I told Tammy that I would be back soon, thinking that this was only a drill. It was just yesterday that we were told that we were not going to be deployed. We all reported to our unit within the required two hours except for some of my soldiers that were partying and drinking at the club. This was their normal practice, just like so many other soldiers after a long day at work. Somehow, they got the word, and they reported in slightly drunk because of the short notice. The truth is many of us thought this was only a drill. We went ahead to the arms room and got our weapons. We thought that it was odd that we were issued live ammo rounds with our weapons. Soon, we started loading up our vehicles and equipment and headed to Rhein- Main Air Force Base near Frankfurt, Germany.

C-5 Galaxy and C-141 transport planes started arriving as soon as we got there. The realization that we were being deployed hit us like a ton of bricks, especially when we started loading our Patriot missile launchers, radar systems, antenna mast group communications system and support equipment on to these waiting jumbo planes with their engine still hot and running. After the equipment was loaded up, we did a head count, received a briefing about our deployment from our battery commander Captain Sam Piper. Our captain never mentioned where we were headed. One soldier asked our captain a question that we all wanted to know.

"Where are we headed, sir?"

He shrugged his shoulders and responded he didn't know.

Our advanced team of soldiers started boarding these colossal transport planes. Many of these soldiers were mine. They were given priority to leave earlier to set up the radar system, communication equipment, and missile launchers and have them ready to launch the missiles with the minimum number of soldiers, time, and equipment and shoot down any incoming enemy aircraft or Scud missiles to the unknown country and location that no one seemed to know or willing to admit that we were headed.

I knew then that my worst nightmare was about to begin. We were in shock. Watching the planes, filled with our soldiers and equipment, taxiing down the runway, we realized that this was not a drill but the real thing. We were really deploying to the war somewhere. Where we were headed, only our senior commanders knew. The sad part, many of us, me included, did not have the opportunity to prepare our families or have the chance to kiss or say goodbye because we all thought this was only a drill. Several hours later after the departure of our first group, I was still at the Rhein- Main Air Force Base waiting for more planes to arrive for the next group of soldiers to leave. I got to thinking why in the world are we deploying so quickly without notice because we are not the 82nd Airborne Division out of Fort Bragg, North Carolina, nor the 101st Airborne Division out of Fort Campbell, Kentucky, or any other rapid deployment force. We were the only soldiers in the Army that I knew of that was deployed without notice like we did, other than the 82nd Airborne Division, 101st Airborne Division, and any other rapid deployment force. Everyone else that left their home bases in preparation for the war had thirty to sixty days to spend with their families after they received the call to be deployed, because they could not arrive in Saudi Arabia before their combat equipment arrived, which was put on planes, railcars, or transport ships.

While we were waiting to go, several of us had the opportunity to call our spouses to let them know that we were really going to war. Now it was my turn to make the call. I was so glad when Tammy answered the phone. By now Tammy was crying because Captain Piper's wife, Carolyn, had already called Tammy and the other spouses with the news that we had already left, going off to war. Tammy was surprised and happy to hear from me. We both were overjoyed with emotion, hearing each other's voices. I had tears in my eyes, and I was trying to stay strong for both of us. We knew that Tammy was due to have our son soon. This was the first time in my life that I felt helpless because there was nothing that I could do to ease her pain. I reminded Tammy that our command had a family support plan that supported our families while we are gone and that someone from our unit will be calling her soon. I kissed her goodbye through the phone, and I told her to tell my kids that I love them and that Daddy will be home soon. I hung the phone up, not knowing if I told the truth or a lie or if I would ever see my family again because I could be killed in the war.

Several of our soldiers were playing cards and other soldiers had on their headphones listening to their music on their portable cassette players while waiting for our turn to ship out. I can remember watching the news on CNN about the activities of the war, when suddenly there was a *breaking news flash* from CNN announcing and showing American troops arriving in Israel. To my surprise, these were my soldiers: fire control operators Sergeant Dennis Malanca, Sergeant Malcolm Weston, Sergeant First Class Robert Walker, and communications Sergeant Carey Collier. They were walking on the landing strip with their M16 rifle drawn across their chest and their duffel bags on their backs.

Several of us started shouting that we were headed to Israel. I was glad but sad at the same time—glad knowing that we were headed to Israel but sad about leaving my family unprepared because of our quick departure. I thought that God does answer prayers. I remembered that I did pray that I would not go to Saudi Arabia, Kuwait, or Iraq. I chuckled to myself that I should had added this to my prayer: "God, please keep me safe, keep me home, and please keep me from the war." By now it was too late. I was already at the air base and at a point of no return.

Soon more C-5 Galaxy and A-141 transport planes were now arriving. It was now our time to board these planes. Prior to boarding, I led a group of soldiers in a prayer for our protection and safety of us and our families. The flight seemed like hours. It was hard to sleep because of the loudness of the plane's engines, the basket-netted cargo seats that we had to sit on, and the uncertainty of what was coming next. Our planes soon arrived at an unknown Israeli air base.

We unloaded the planes and boarded the back ends of our deuce- and-a-half cargo trucks while other soldiers drove our vehicles loaded with our equipment to unknown destination. We noticed, while in route to our destination, that the air raid sirens were going off. These sirens sounded just like our twelve o'clock noon whistles and our tornado sirens back home. We were later told through our combat radios that Israel was undergoing two Scud missile attacks. Minutes later, upon our arrival at this location, we were told that we were in Haifa.

We deployed from Germany to the nation of Israel as part of joint task force Patriot missiles in defense of the nation of Israel. My unit, Alpha Battery 4/43 Air Defense Artillery, commanded by Capt. Sam Piper, was assigned to protect the population, strategic sites, and skies over Haifa. Our other sister units—Bravo Battery, which was commanded by Captain Woods, and Charlie Battery, commanded by Capt. Joe Foster—were both were assigned to protect the same areas at Tel Aviv. We also had our headquarters' battery and our 518th Maintenance Support Company assigned to Tel Aviv as well. The Netherlands, or the Dutch, was also part of the joint task force Patriot missiles. They were assigned to protect the population, strategic sites, and skies over Jerusalem. We had an unknown mission, assigned by God, to protect the children of Father Abraham. These are the Christians, Muslims, and Jews—all citizens of Israel— living in these areas.

My unit was assigned to an Israeli base. We stayed in the only barrack that was there. Our sister units were assigned to the open fields in Tel Aviv. This meant that we stayed in a barrack while they had to live in tents. They stayed in what we called tent city. Within hours, we were all set up and ready to defend our areas of responsibilities. Our Air Defense Artillery motto was "If it flies, it dies." We were ready and prepared to prove to the world that the Patriot missiles would do exactly what we were sent to do. Our mission was to defend and shoot down every Scud missile that Saddam Hussein and his generals would be bold enough to fire at the nation of Israel.

Patriot soldiers in Tel Aviv

After several days in Haifa, I felt safe and spiritually protected, even after we came under several Scud missile attacks. The spirit in me told me that this was a divine set up by God for us to be there. It was in God's plan all along to keep us in Germany while every other Patriot missile battalion was deployed to the Gulf region. God picked the appointed time to send us to Israel. Our God-ordained mission was to protect the Holy Land against the most dreaded weapon in Iraq's war arsenal, the Al Hussein Scud missile. Out of all the Patriot units in the United States Army, God chose us to protect Israel. We were the last, but the best, Patriot missile battalion sent to the war. God chose Lieutenant Colonel Krimkowitz, a Jewish officer, in advance of the war to be our battalion commander.

I felt the presence of the Holy Spirit and a hand on my shoulder when I came to the realization that God also chose me, an American Christian soldier and an ambassador for Christ, to be in Israel as part of a team that was chosen by Him to protect God's people. I was proud to be a representative of the United States Army and the United

States of America, but most importantly, I was representing Christ in Israel. I knew then that there was something that God wanted me to experience, write about, and share with the world after the war is over. I asked myself if this was the mission that God had pick me for. Amen.

Iraq fired eighty-eight Scud missiles during the entire Gulf War. Forty-two of these Scud missiles were fired at the nation of Israel. Thirty-four of these missiles were fired at Israel while we were there. Iraq tried to split the coalition by launching Scud missiles into Israel. Saddam Hussein's and his general's master plan and part of his strategy was to get Israel involved in the war. Their plan would have splintered the coalition that included ten Arab or Muslim countries. None of them wanted to be known in history as fighting on the side of their common and historical enemy, the Jews, against a fellow Arab or Muslim country.

Every night and every time from January 18 until the end of the war, a Scud missile was fired toward either Kuwait, Saudi Arabia, or Israel. The air raid sirens would sound in every one of these countries indicating that a Scud missile had just been fired and was in flight. This prompted us to go into our bomb shelters. The Israeli citizens had to go into their sealed rooms in their homes. Every Israeli, including the infant and elderly, were given an emergency kit that included a gas mask and auto atropine injector. The auto atropine injector was to be administered in the event Iraq used chemical warheads on the Scud missile. The auto atropine injector was only to be used if chemicals from the Scud missile attack were detected. I learned years later that 222 Israelis were hospitalized because they panicked and accidently took the auto atropine injector on some of these Scud missile attacks.

Going into these bomb shelters and the sealed rooms was necessary because it was too hard to determine initially where the Scud missile was headed. Every time that we went into a shelter, we had to put on our hot chemical protective suits and put on our M-17A1 protective gas mask. We all had to put on these masks because the Scud missile had the capability to be fitted with a chemical warhead. Saddam Hussein had used chemical weapons in the past, against Iran and his own Kurdish people. Surely, he would not hesitate to use them against his enemy, the Jewish people. Everyone had to stay in these shelters until the Scud missile was either destroyed, knocked off its course, or until the Scud missile hit its intended target. On January 25, a week after our arrival, Iraq fired seven Scud missiles in one day at Haifa and Tel Aviv. Our missile batteries at each of these locations engaged and destroyed six of the seven incoming Scud missiles. Near Tel Aviv, one Scud missile was damaged when it was hit by a Patriot missile. One Israeli citizen was killed and forty-two others were wounded by the falling debris from a Scud missile.

On February 5, I celebrated my thirty-third birthday by myself in Israel. I had a piece of cake and some Jell-O. I was given the opportunity to call my family. The kids were happy to hear from me. They sang "Happy Birthday." This made my day. I placed a second call to my mother. This was the first time that I spoke to her since going to war. It has always been my practice to call her on my birthday to thank her for having me. She was happy to hear from me. We prayed for our safety. On February 16, Tammy went into labor and was rushed to the German hospital in a town called Lich by Captain Piper's wife, Carolyn Piper. Our German neighbors looked after our kids until someone from our unit came to take them.

On the next day, February 17, my son, Lloyd Calvin Glover Jr., was born. He was born five years to the day when my daughter Latasha was born. I got the call from my commander that he was born that evening. I later learned that Tammy was not alone in the delivery room. One of our German neighbors was with her during the birth of our son. I was overcome by emotions when I got the news. Every soldier in my unit congratulated me, and we all celebrated his birth. Even though my son was born in a German hospital, he was still an American citizen born abroad. I prayed and thanked God that they both were safe. Kim Overton, the wife of our motor pool sergeant, Leon Overton, volunteered to take care of my three older kids for eight days while Tammy was in the hospital recovering from childbirth. She had to remain in the hospital until my son was circumcised,. which is customary for baby boys born in Germany.

Tammy's friend Joyce Gomez picked up my kids from Kim's house and bought them to the hospital to visit my wife and newborn son. Tammy and I were forever grateful to Kim for taking care of our kids. Our families became good friends, and we are still best of friends even to this day. We often forget of the stress that the family members that remain behind must endure as a result of their loved one being deployed to a war. Let us not forget that they, too, pay a price of war. They are unsung heroes.

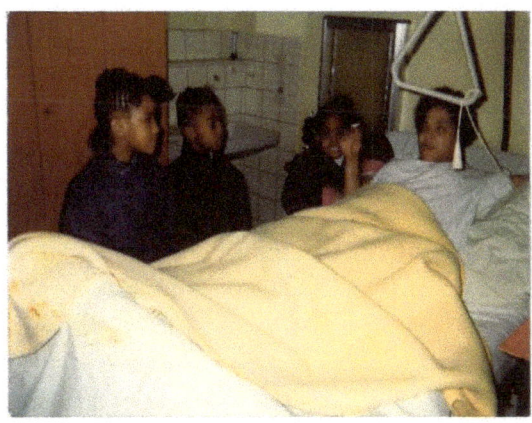

Tammy and the kids at the German hospital

On February 24, the ground war started. Thing started to get more intense. Iraq started firing more Scud missiles in response to the ground war at Saudi Arabia, Kuwait, Israel, and also one at Bahrain and one at Qatar. We found ourselves going inside these dreaded bomb shelters at least two to three times a day. I was asked by several of our soldiers to pray, and I would pray openly for our safety and protection each time that we were under a Scud missile attack. When we were under Scud missile attack, we would sit inside these bomb shelters with these M17A1 protective mask on for like hours but really, it was only half hour at best each time.

Wearing these masks and hot chemical protective suits that we call MOPP suits (mission oriented protective posture), which were designed to be worn in a toxic environment during a chemical, biological, radiological, or a nuclear attack for twenty minutes or more was difficult at best. The fear of a Scud missile attack overhead added more pressure in this demanding situation. The bomb shelter was hot. There was no good airflow. Every soldier on our site that was not manning the equipment or on guard duty had to report to this shelter for accountability. It was hot, difficult to breathe at times, and difficult to see because of the fogging of the lenses on your mask.

We would sit in the darkness of these shelters feeling helpless and silent while these sirens were sounding until our commander gave the command of "All clear." This command was given by our commander indicating that the missile attack was over. We were all glad to hear the words "All clear." These two words let us know that the missile attack was over. This allowed us to remove our gas mask and chemical suits and allowed us to leave the bomb shelters to get the much-needed fresh air. This also allowed us to return to our duty assignments. We soon learned that during the first week of the ground war that one of our former infantry soldiers who was assigned to our

74

Patriot unit, Sergeant Smith, was one of the soldiers killed on the first days of combat in Kuwait. Many of us that knew him personally was devastated by the news. We all remembered him as a tough and gung-ho soldier that loved being an infantry soldier. He made it known that he loved serving his country.

There were times when the radar system would suddenly alarm and turn in the direction of an incoming Scud missile and several of us who are outside performing system checks would be caught off guard. You would hear the thunderous sounds of the Patriot missile's engines starting up and then see the blast flames of several Patriot missiles suddenly being launched. Talking about being scared and seeing your life flash before you. The missile launchers were down range, away from us. We were not in danger to the blast. The problem was that if one of these missiles would have misfired, we could had been injured or we could had been exposed to the radiation that was emitted from the high-powered radar system that communicated with the missiles guidance system during launch. We really did not know how this exposure would affect us. We got checked out later by medical staff. Everything medically was okay with us.

I was especially proud as the fire control platoon sergeant when my soldiers had 100 percent successful engagements of every incoming Scud missile that were projected to hit our missile site or nearby on one of the Haifa's population city centers or at one of their strategic sites. Sergeant Weston was credited with having the first engagement in shooting down the first Scud missile that was headed to the Haifa area. My fire control operators, led by Sergeant First Class Walker, Sergeant Malanca, and Sergeant Weston, and my communication sergeant Staff Sergeant Collier all received Bronze Star Medals or Meritorious Service Medals along with many of our soldiers for their actions during the war.

Our actions saved Israeli lives and helped end the Gulf War. It is a proven fact that our unit, commanded by Capt. Sam Piper, had a 100 percent kill rate against incoming Scud missiles that were headed to the Haifa area. The following day after a Scud missile attack, the citizens of Haifa would show up outside our gates to thank us for protecting the skies around them. They would bring cookies, cakes, candies, and all kinds of Israeli desserts to us to show their appreciation. Many of them took pictures with us and some of them asked and received autographs from us too. There were days during the war that they would send entertainers to our site, the Israeli version of the USO, to put on shows to make us feel at home.

Israeli citizens at our missile site

We also had a famous Israeli defense force officer, Captain Rafi, who worked alongside our crew. He earned his fame as an officer in 1983 when he shot down a Syrian MIG-25 during Israel's Peace for Galilee operation in Lebanon. As an Israeli officer that engaged and shot down several Scud missiles that were headed to Haifa's areas added to his fame as a national hero. One of the quick lessons that we learned was that all the Scud missiles attacks would occur only at night. This made it difficult for the fighter jets to discover their locations because the Scud launcher could move in the darkness of the night.

My Relationship with God in Haifa

It was good being in Haifa during the war. Of course, we would have preferred to be back home in Germany with our families. There were many benefits of being assigned to Haifa. Most importantly, we stayed in a barrack and not outside in tents like our sister batteries did in Tel Aviv. We had the luxury of taking hot showers; a TV to watch the news, mostly about what was going on in the war; a landline phone to periodically call our spouses; a dining facility that was staffed by Israeli cooks that served three great meals per day plus nighttime snacks. I wanted to improve my health, so I chose to eat a lot of tuna fish and sardines. We also had a small store in the barrack and another larger one on this site that was set up for us to buy snacks, writing materials, Israeli postcards, and personal hygiene items.

By this time, we started receiving letters from schoolchildren from Israel and the United States, thanking us for being in the Army and protecting them in the war. Many of them had pictures that they drew of themselves that made us smile and laugh. This made a lot of us feel good and important too. We also had several amateur barbers that volunteered, and some of them charged five dollars to keep us looking good even in war. My chosen barber was Specialist Keith Weathers. His specialty was a bowl-styled haircut without a good bowl. He made you look like a good-looking Marine. The other barbers that cut our White brothers' hair could not cut hair at all. We used to laugh so hard every time one of them cut someone else's hair. After several weeks of bad haircuts, they finally got it right.

These luxuries and benefits, along with having weekly Bible studies and church services, added to our morale, especially when we were able to call home and talk with our families. I also had another opportunity to call my mother back in New Jersey. She was so happy to hear from me. She loved and was proud of the fact that we were in Israel. Mom said that we will be blessed by God for serving in Israel. We also spoke about what was going on with my family and friends in New Jersey. Mom prayed with me for our safety and our safe return.

We were fortunate to have Bible studies and church services at our site that were conducted by our Army chaplain, Captain Dugal. Captain Dugal was a Methodist seminary-trained chaplain. He was incredibly good at conducting services and speaking one on one with soldiers that needed his counseling services. During the war, whenever he conducted church services, the room was full of soldiers needing spiritual guidance from him and comfort from the war. Staff Sergeant Gadson and I would help him out whenever and whatever ways we could to help him conduct these services. During the war, every soldier was given the opportunity to attend these services. Many of them made the choice to attend these services if they were not pulling guard duty or manning the equipment.

Staff Sergeant Gadson and I would meet on occasions when we had time to discuss topics in the Bible and discuss matters about our church back in Germany. This discussion included the health and welfare of our church families. This deployment was a little difficult for him because he was recently appointed our pastor ten months prior to our deployment. Staff Sergeant Gadson, who I also called Pastor Gadson and my friend, had a pastoral love for our church members. I could look in his eyes and sense the pain that he was going through for not being there in Giessen with the church families. Many of our church families had either a husband or a wife that deployed to the war. I believe he would have preferred to be back in Giessen, shepherding the church members that remained in Giessen.

It was difficult for us to meet as much or as often as we would have like to because of our work schedules. I oversaw my Patriot fire control platoon while he directed his infantry squad. My platoon was like the watchmen in Ezekiel 33:7 (NIV) with the responsibilities for watching the skies over Haifa and the surrounding areas for any incoming Scud missile attacks. If an incoming Scud missile were detected in our area of responsibility by our radar system, my soldiers had the task of identifying, engaging, and operating the fire control mechanisms that would have launched the Patriot missile and shot down the incoming Scud missile. Staff Sergeant Gadson worked in our command post. He oversaw our infantry squad. His infantry squad had the responsibility for the security of our missile site. They had to be prepared to quickly repel any potential ground attack from the enemy. The enemy could have been any of the terrorist groups from the Gaza strip, Syria, Jordan, Iraq, or any other country around the world that did not like the United States.

About every day I would go to my secret place, which was outside within the fence of our missile site. I would walk, talk, pray to God, and listen for his voice. I had to do this outside the barrack because there were no designated quite spaces within the barrack for me to spend private time with God. Being in Israel on Mount Carmel, of all places in the Bible, protecting the citizens of Israel gave me a greater spiritual connection and closeness with God. Many days I felt his awesome presence. I would talk and listen for the Abba Father to whisper to my spirit. God confirmed to me in my spirit during one of these quiet time talks with Him that me and everyone else from my unit would live and not die in this war and that our families back in Germany and those families that went back to the United States will all be safe during the war. God whispered to my spirit that this will happen because I have been faithful and because I asked him too in my prayers along with many faithful believers of Christ and because He alone had chosen our battalion to protect the children of Israel.

I knew then that we were God's battle-axes; and He was watching over our units in Haifa, Tel Aviv, and Jerusalem like a father eagle watching over his young eaglets. I did a praise dance with all my might like King David did in 2 Samuel 6:14 but with my Army uniform on. I was so happy with the revelation, confirmation, and blessing from God that I shouted out in the open field, "Abba Father" and God's name "Jehovah-Jireh, the Provider," and "Hallelujah." Several of my soldiers that were nearby doing system checks and maintenance on the radar system heard me and looked up at me. One soldier was smiling so hard. He asked me with joy in his eyes, "Was he here yet?" He was thinking of my son soon to be born. I laughed with the biggest smile. I responded to him, "No, not yet, soldier. No, not yet."

One of these evenings I was lying in my bed trying to relax from the war and the difficulties of being away from my family, the thought of Tammy being alone with my three kids and about to deliver my son any day without me being there, and the uncertainties of war. My eyes were open, but I was not sleep. I know this might sound crazy to you, but I suddenly felt my body drifting as if I was leaving my body, but I was still in my body. The room was slightly dark when suddenly there appeared a half-opened door with a bright light illuminating from it. A baby crawled from beneath my bed in a dark-colored hooded robe with its face and head hidden under the hood. It appeared out of nowhere in my room. The baby started crawling fast toward the half-open door with a bright light illuminating from it. I got scared for the baby, so I followed it into the slightly open door. I pushed opened the door, which opened into an extremely large and beautiful hallway of a castle.

The hallway was immaculate and beautiful with the largest ceiling that I ever saw. The floor was covered with beautiful thick glass floor. As I looked down at the glass floor, I could see myself looking down at the floor, and

81

underneath the floor, I could see the sky and the clouds dancing under it. I got a little dizzy at first because I really thought that I was really walking over a twenty-four-foot-wide view of the heavens below. The wall that was in front of me was a crimson-colored wall that covered with gold and shiny bronze stones, and in the middle of the wall was the most beautiful twelve-by- twelve-foot portrait. There was amazing music that was coming from it. The instrumental sounds were so beautiful to my ears that I couldn't describe them with human words.

The portrait was perfectly centered on the wall. It was alive with water, blood, and fire, glowing and dancing around inside it. The baby had stopped crawling about twelve feet in front of the picture and was looking up at the picture too. He turned around toward me as if he were waiting for me. I picked the baby up so that we could get a closer and better look together at the portrait. I also glanced at the baby's face and slightly pulled back his hood as we moved closer to the portrait. I was stunned when I looked at the baby's face. It was me. A baby me with a light-bronze complexion with beautiful long, wavy black baby hair.

I asked myself and God, "What in the name of Jesus is going on?" As we moved closer to the portrait, the portrait transformed into a mirror, and the baby transformed in my arms to a child in a white robe, now around eight years old, but this time with beautiful woolly, curly black hair. The child, still in the white robe and now getting too heavy for me to carry, jumped out of my arms and ran away. I walked closer to the mirror to get a better look. When I got closer, I could see someone in a white robe with beautiful woolly, curly black hair. He looked just like the child that ran away and was now looking at me, mirroring my every step. I got closer to the portrait, and I saw that the person in the mirror looked just like me, but a beautiful, majestic me with beautiful woolly, curly black hair. I was stunned, so I started slowly backing

82

away. He started to back away too. When I moved to the left, he moved to the left. When I moved to the right, he moved to the right. By now I was so scared but not frightened to the point that I thought I was going to die from a heart attack, so I then backed away from the mirror. The farther I got away from the mirror, the mirror would transform back into the picture with the water, blood, and fire glowing and dancing in it.

Boy! Talking about really being scared, so I trotted down the long glass-covered hallway. I could see an evening sky with glittering stars as I looked downward. I trotted toward the only door that was slightly open, which had light coming out from it. When I got closer to the door, I could hear what sounded like a choir singing. I pushed open the heavy gold-cover castle door that led me outside into the entrance of a huge coliseum full to its capacity with tens of thousands of people dressed in white robes singing and looking upward toward the sky. Just around the same time that I entered into the coliseum, I could hear the blast of many trumpets sounding, and the people all stood up and started clapping, shouting, and singing in an endless chorus in tongues that sounded like tongues of a million angelic beings. I was happy because I thought that they were clapping for me because I was victorious in completing some type of supernatural test or trial. I then looked up toward the sky to see what they were looking at and clapping for. There appeared eight colossal purple lions with gold crowns covered with diamonds on their heads. It was the lions that they were really singing too. The lions' combined width was the length of the coliseum.

They were slowly descending from the clouds as if they were Army paratroopers guiding themselves into the coliseum or like airborne soldiers prepared for battle but without the parachutes guiding them in and without rifles on their side. I then heard a voice within my spirit that told to me that they are shouting and singing, "Yahweh, hallelujah. Yahweh, hallelujah." The lions started roaring in unisons. The last words that I heard in my spirit was the roaring of the lions and the crowd singing "Hallelujah." At that moment my dream, vision, or whatever that was ended because I got interrupted by those damn air raid sirens that were now sounding. I could feel myself drifting back to my body.

I got mad as hell, picked up my weapon, and I went ahead to my fire control center to make sure that my soldiers were ready for any incoming Scud missiles. They were battle ready as always, so I went ahead to the bomb shelter. The missile was fired at Saudi Arabia instead. Our Patriot unit in Saudi Arabia destroyed the Scud missile in the air. As soon as we got an all clear. I accounted for all my soldiers and then conducted some of my platoon sergeant duties. Once I was done, I then proceeded back to my room hoping that I could return and finish what had occurred prior to the air raid sirens sounding. To my disappointment, my dream never returned. I did not know what to make of this, so I recorded it in my sergeant's notebook that I carried around with me so that I could transcribed it later in my prayer journal.

Tragedy in Dhahran and the End of the Gulf War

On February 25, tragedy struck in Saudi Arabia when a Patriot missile battery failed to engage an incoming Scud missile. The Scud missile slammed into a makeshift barrack in Dhahran, Saudi Arabia, killing at least 28 soldiers and injuring up to 110 soldiers from a Pennsylvania Army reserve unit. An investigation was conducted days later. It determined that the Patriot's radar system failed. We all felt the pain of the loss of these soldiers too because of the role the Patriot missile system played in this disaster. We prayed for the soldiers and their families during our next church service. We also prayed for the soldiers of that Patriot unit as well.

It was heart breaking, as a Patriot soldier, to hear on the news people criticizing about this one Patriot missile failure and already declaring its defeat. Little did they, or the world, know that the Patriot missile was originally designed to shoot down fighter jets, not long-range tactical ballistic Scud missiles. If the Patriot missile destroyed the missile in the air or knocked the Scud missile off its intended course, it was considered a success. The length of a Scud missile is 36.9 feet long compared to the nineteen-foot-long Patriot missile. In other words, it was like David versus Goliath. If you really think about it, the Patriot missile was that smooth stone in David's slingshot that killed Goliath in 1 Samuel 17:48–51.

Goliath was the terror weapon used by the enemy, the Philistines, against the children of Israel back in the days of young David. Today the Scud missile was that terror weapon used by Israel's enemy, Iraq. This might be the first time that you have heard this. The Patriot missile, just like that smooth stone used by David, was the weapon that threw a death blow to Saddam Hussein's battle plans to have Israel join the war, with the purpose of dividing the coalition. That is why our God, the God of Father Abraham, held the soldiers of 4/43 Air Defense Artillery with His chosen Jewish commander back in Germany until Iraq fired its first Scud missile attack at Israel. Isn't God's plan great? God deserves to hear you shout, "Hallelujah" and "Amen!"

On February 27, President George Bush announced that the war was over. We all celebrated the good news. After forty-one days of the aerial war, after forty days of us being in Israel, and after a one hundred hours of ground war in the desert and the terror of those Scud missile attacks, the war came to a quick ending. The desert war that Saddam Hussein said that would be the "mother of all battles" fizzled and never happened at the level that he boasted about because of the Patriot missile and our battlefield coalition of soldiers, airmen, sailors, Marines. The thought of me dying as one of those 213 out of the 425 soldiers that the Army chaplain told us that would die and the thought of me being that soldier that died in battle with a newborn baby on the way never happened.

The first chance that I got, I thanked God with a big "Hallelujah," and I told Him how much I loved Him. Next, I called Tammy with the good news. We were both happy knowing that I would be coming home soon. The promises that God made to me was true. None of our soldiers died, and our families were safe too. We did have one of our sergeants, who was in Tele Aviv, hurt pretty bad during a mobility incident. He was airlifted back to Germany for lifesaving treatment. He survived the incident and had a productive military career after the incident. I felt great knowing that my relationship with God and my prayers and the prayers of other believers made us safe. We celebrated our victory over Iraq. The next day the citizens of Haifa came out to our site and celebrated with us too.

The moment that President Bush announced that the war was over, our first and only casualty came in the form of our church service. It was a little disappointing that only around thirty-two soldiers participated in our first church service after President Bush made the announcement. Our church service participation went from an attendance of seventy-five to around thirty-two soldiers that week. In the following weeks, the participation gradually dropped and remained steady to around six die-hard soldiers, which included me and Staff Sergeant Gadson, until our last days in Israel. The threat of the war and the thought of dying was no longer a concern to the soldiers that no longer attended or felt the need of steady prayer and comfort of a group setting. My only prayer and hope are that every one of them will continue to attend services and remember how they needed the protection and presence of God during the war once they return to Germany.

We also quickly learned that we were not going anywhere yet. There were over six hundred thousand soldiers that were still in the Gulf region, mostly in Saudi Arabia and Kuwait, that participated in Operation Desert Shield, now Operations Desert Storm. Most of them are by now victorious battle-hardened soldiers that have been over there in the desert for six months since August 1990. It took several months to get all those soldiers and equipment over to the Gulf region, and it will take time to reverse the process. It was understandable that they had a higher priority to return home to their families than we had. We all accepted the fact that we were going to remain in Israel for another several months. We also realized that Saddam Hussein was still in power and still was the murderous dictator of Iraq. He still had those hidden Scud missiles and those other weapons of mass destruction. We had to be prepared to counter any Scud missiles if he decided to go against the peace discussion and to attack Israel again. Just knowing that we were still alive and safe in Israel made the wait well worth it. I had to call Tammy with the disappointing news that we were not coming home anytime soon. This meant that I had to wait longer to see my fourth gift from God, my newborn son, Lloyd Calvin Glover Jr.

Remaining in Israel a little longer wasn't so bad. To help pass the time away, we were given permission to leave our missile site to visit the shopping areas, restaurant, beaches, gyms, and recreation centers and sites around the city of Haifa. Several of us were given permission to jog on the streets of Haifa. I would spend most of my free time jogging and listening to my portable cassette player with my headphones on. I loved listening to the gospel music of James Cleveland, John P. Kee, and the Williams brothers. I would run by myself for miles, looking at the scenery of Mount Carmel, shopping centers, and the neighborhood landscaping that surround this historical city. Some of those days I would run to the Haifa family recreation center and gym. I would see many of our soldiers there. They were either there relaxing or working out. They drove to these locations in Army vehicles while I ran the distance of six miles to get there. It usually took me an hour to run there.

I really cherished the moments when while running on the streets of Haifa, the citizens of Haifa would notice me running. Many of them would stop with their families and point, wave, and say *shalom* and *toda raba* to me, which means "Hello" and "Thank you very much" in Hebrew. It was obvious to everyone that I ran past them that I was one of those American soldiers, known to them as a Scud buster, who protected them during the war. I would wave back at them and say, "Shalom, toda raba," right back to them. I would then add, "Yom tov" (Hebrew word for "Have a good day.") I learned this from a Jewish teenager that I spoke with at the family recreation center. I would feel a runner's high or rush of adrenaline knowing that I was running the streets of Israel. Yes, I would talk and listen for God. Running has also been one of my best private

88

times with God. When I am running, I could see the beauty of His holiness and wave at His creations.

On one of those days, I was asked by my First Sergeant James Hereford if I was willing to take a group of our soldiers to visit the children's hospital in Haifa. I jumped at the opportunity to do this. I took fifteen soldiers with me. It was heartwarming to see the young children in these hospital wards. Many of them had serious or terminal illnesses. They were happy to see us and to take pictures with us as well. The love that we felt and the respect that we received were mutual. The hospital staff was great too. They thanked us for cheering up the kids and them too. My only regret was that I didn't bring a camera and was not able to take my own pictures. I am sad to mention this, but I must. It was sad to see that every one of these children, regardless of their young ages, had their Israeli-made gas mask near their bedsides.

On another occasion, I was invited along with Staff Sergeant Gadson to a Jewish kibbutz to attend the Jewish festival of Purim. A kibbutz is a small community that comprises of several hundred residents. The kibbutz and its income—at least, traditionally—comes from agriculture and industry. The residents are referred to as kibbutzniks. They work on dairy farms, in orchards, and even outside their kibbutz. Everyone there contributes their full paychecks into the communal pot. Everyone receives an equal monthly share from the kibbutz's administration regardless of what they do or how much money they put into the fund.

This story is recounted in the Old Testament book of Esther. Esther records the institution of the annual festival of Purim through the historical account of Esther, a Jewish girl who became Queen of Persia and saved her people from destruction. The story recounts how the feast of Purim came to be celebrated by the Jews. Esther, the beautiful Jewish wife of the Persian king Ahasuerus, and her cousin Mordecai persuaded the king to retract an order calling for the general annihilation of Jews throughout the Persian Empire. The massacre had been plotted by the king's chief minister, Haman, and the date was decided by casting lots (*Purim*). Instead of the destructions of the Jews, Haman himself was hanged on the planned date and on the gallows that he had built for the hanging of Mordecai, according to the book of Esther. The feast of Purim was established to celebrate this day ("Purim: Definition, Story, History, Traditions, and Facts," *Britannica*).

We had an amazing time watching the play about this festival of Purim and listening to the music and speeches that were given. The food was fantastic. I was especially touched when the leader of the kibbutz introduced us by name and thanked us for being American Scud busters. It was a great feeling, and I was especially proud when the citizens of the Kibbutz gave us a standing ovation. We were both given an invite to come back anytime as their guest. We left that evening very appreciative of the Jewish culture. I was so happy to see the story of Esther played out in a play. I spend the next several days reading the ten chapters of the book of Esther for a better understanding.

A Navy battleship that saw action in the Gulf War had come into dock at the naval port in Haifa to replenish much-needed supplies and for ship repairs. We were given the opportunity to tour their battleship and to eat lunch on this massive and impressive ship. We also had the opportunity to watch the sailor play with the Marines in a fun basketball game on the hanger of this ship. Their sailors, the Marines, and officers also had the opportunity to tour and eat lunch at our missile site as well. We were all impressed by what we saw on their ship, and they were impressed on what they saw on our missile site.

I was proud to see on the news the soldiers, airmen, sailors, and Marines return to their home bases in the United States as heroes with parades and welcome-home ceremonies. I must admit that it has always been a childhood dream of mine, especially when I played army with Brian and my other friends growing up, that I would go off to war and return home to the roars of a cheering crowd of the ticker-tape parade as a returning hometown war hero and a Medal of Honor awardee in Plainfield.

The war was over. I knew then that my dream was just a pipe dream, and it was not going to happen. I also came to the realization that I left Plainfield fifteen years ago, right after my high school graduation in June of 1976, and that very few people in Plainfield, outside my family, knew that I was still alive, still in the Army, and, most importantly to me, that I participated in the Gulf War.

I often wondered and would say to myself that it would have been nice to know if my hometown was aware that they had two of their own native sons participate in the Gulf War. I am sure that there were other soldiers from Plainfield that participated in the Gulf War too. But I only knew of myself; Specialist Leonard Goodson, who was younger than me; and our Army combat medic, who was the other Plainfield native son in my unit. Plainfield had two newspapers, the *Plainfield Courier News* and the *Newark Star Ledger*. I felt that they could or would have mentioned our service had they known. We were still in Israel, waiting our time to return home to our families in Germany. I often wondered how we would be received and welcomed back in Germany upon our return too.

By now it was late March, the snow was falling heavily in Germany. I was concerned with the fact that Tammy now had four kids that she had to pack up in our car to travel back and forth to the commissary and the post exchange in Giessen to buy food and much-needed supplies. Tammy also had to go by our barrack to get mail, my bimonthly pay statements, and to receive updated information from our rear detachment commander about our redeployment. It was hard to understand that no one in our chain of command had a confirmed date for our return to Germany. I made it a point to call Tammy every three days or when I could to speak to her and my four kids. Just hearing their young voices and the sounds of my newborn son in the background was enough to keep me happy and motivated. I would also look at their pictures and smile, knowing that I would be with them soon. There were days that I felt homesick, and I would hold their pictures next to my heart and ask the Holy Spirit to whisper to Tammy and their young hearts that I would be home soon.

Haifa had its famous Bible sites as well. The cave of Elijah was located within several miles from our missile site. I visited the cave of Elijah twice to get a better understanding of what took place at this site, which is recorded in the Old Testament book of I Kings. Elijah's cave is one of the most sacred caves in the Holy Land. According to the tradition of all faiths (Jews, Christians, Muslims, and Druze), it was one of the places where Prophet Elijah had lived and hid while operating around Mount Carmel twenty-nine centuries ago. Visitors come to the cave to pray daily, and there are large ceremonies held several times a year.

My Last Days in the Holy Land

We finally got the word that we were leaving Israel sometime within the next two or three weeks in April. This gave us hope and time to visit some of the other historical sites in Israel. The first day we were able to travel happened on March 31, which was on Easter Sunday. It was a special treat for us to go to Capernaum, which is called the Town of Jesus. This is the town where Jesus performed over forty miracles, including healing the sick and even raising people from the dead, according to Matthew 8:5, Mark 2:1–12, Luke 7:1–10, and Luke17–26. It was nice riding on buses, looking at the scenery of the towns that we passed on our way to Capernaum. As soon as we arrived at Capernaum, we got off our buses. We were instructed to assemble on a popular hillside overlooking the Sea of Galilee. This hillside is believed to be the area where Jesus conducted the historical Sermon on the Mount. The Sermon on the Mount refers to the longest recorded sermon by Jesus found in the Bible. It was recorded in Matthew 5–7. Jesus was summarizing the right ways for us to approach God and to deal with other people. One of the Bible verses that Jesus said during the Sermon of the Mount touched my soul: "The truly fortunate and blessed people are those who are rich in the things that matter to God, not those who have money, power, popularity or fame."

We were assembled on this hillside to participate in a sermon that was to be conducted by our chaplain Dugal. Chaplain Dugal started out by telling us about the significance of Capernaum, the Sermon of the Mount, and the schedule of our activities that day. Next, he conducted a beautiful sermon using the same message of the Beatitudes found in Matthew 5–7. It was interesting listening to his sermon and how it must have sounded while Jesus conducted the same Sermon on the Mount while preaching to the multitudes that numbered in the thousands without a microphone and speakers. I can see how the natural sounds and the acoustic of this hillside made this possible for everyone to hear. I also noticed that there were tourists that had also gathered around us, and they, too, were listening and enjoying Chaplain Dugal's rendition of Jesus's Sermon on the Mount. They all clapped when he finished his sermon.

Chaplain Dugal conducted a beautiful sermon that ended with the announcement that our next stop would be to the Yardenit baptismal pool, which is the most important and famous baptismal site for Christian pilgrims and one of the many holy sites around the Sea of Galilee, Capernaum, Tabgha, and Mount of Beatitudes. Chaplain Dugal also said that anyone that wanted to be baptized could be baptized in the Sea of Galilee. I believed that everyone that chose to would be baptized regardless of their understanding and relationship with our Savior.

We arrived at the baptismal pool that had water flowing from the Sea of Galilee. We changed our clothes, and we were given white baptismal robes that we were required to be baptized in. Chaplain Dugal spoke on the importance of being baptized and why it is necessary for all of us as a Christian to be saved and then baptized. Chaplain Dugal was assisted by Staff Sergeant Gadson and by another minister to conduct these baptismal. I was baptized when I was ten years old before by Pastor Dodge with my brothers and sisters. The Lutheran church, like many denominations, baptized by sprinkling water over your head. This was an opportunity to be submerged in water; and the thought of being baptized in Israel, in the Yardenit baptismal pool, which has water flowing from the Sea of Galilee, was too hard to let this opportunity pass me by. So, I got baptized for the second time. It was a special blessing for me, and it was also beautiful watching my fellow soldiers getting baptized too. I do believe that several of my

94

fellow soldiers were not saved but got baptized anyway for the purpose of saying that they were baptized in the Sea of Galilee, not realizing how their lives could be changed. I realized that the Holy Spirit would have to step in. It was not my assignment to convict them because it is the ministry of the Holy Spirit to convict and save those that needed to be saved. Later, everyone that got baptized received a baptismal certificate as proof that we were baptized in the Jordan River on March 31, 1991. It was a certificate that we would cherish forever. Amen.

Baptismal pool

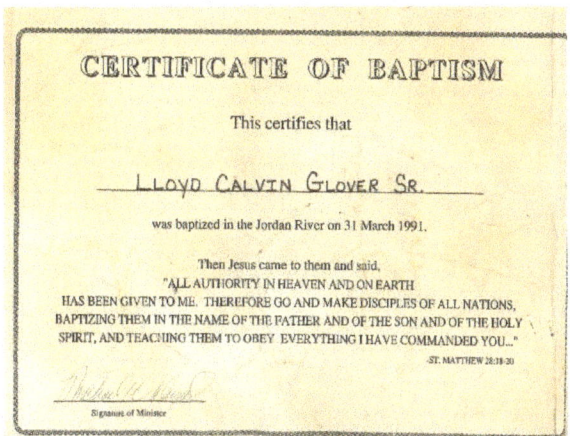

Baptismal certificates

95

After all the baptismal were completed, we changed back into our Army uniforms. We then headed over to the Church of the Beatitudes. The Church of the Beatitudes is a Roman Catholic church located on the Mount of Beatitudes. This is a beautiful church. We were able to look at its architect, the painting, and historical surrounding depicting the days of Jesus. There was a gift store inside the church; and many of our soldiers bought merchandise, gifts, and postcards to send back to their families. We then left the church area and walked around Capernaum, taking pictures. It was especially heartwarming to know that we were walking around and looking around the area of the Sea of Galilee, the same place that every year, thousands of Christians come to explore the place where Jesus spent his life and where he gave the Sermon on the Mount and to see the synagogues where he taught and preached as well as the site of many of His miracles (which included the miracle of the five loaves and fishes wherein He fed the five thousand with five loaves and two fish, according to John 6:12–13, and of Jesus walking on water, which was recorded in Matthew 14:22–33).

I took two priceless pictures that will remain with me for the rest of my life and will be passed down to future generations to serve as a historical proof that their grandfather visited and walked around the same places that our Lord and Savior had walked and lived. The first picture is one that I took with Sergeant Weston and Specialist Weathers. We stood in front of the sign that said, "Welcome to Capernaum, the Town of Jesus," and the second picture is one I took with Chaplain Dugal and Staff Sergeant Gadson with the Sea of Galilee as a backdrop. I love these two pictures, but the one with Chaplain Dugal and Staff Sergeant Gadson was precious to me because all three of us were ministers and soldiers for Christ.

Welcome to Capernaum

SGT Weston, SFC Glover and SPC Weathers

SSG Gadson, CPT Dugal and SFC Glover
Sea of Galilee

Next, we got on tourist boats that took us across the Sea of Galilee to a restaurant that served St. Peter's fish. St. Peter's fish is a specialty that every tourist wants to eat. In Matthew 14:13–21, Jesus tells Peter to go fishing in the Sea of Galilee and the first fish he'd caught would have a silver shekel in its mouth, which Peter could use to pay the Temple tax. Peter followed Christ's instructions, and indeed, the fish he caught had a shekel in its mouth. Peter then paid the Temple tax, which allowed Jesus and his disciples to enter the Temple. According to legend, the fish Peter caught was a tilapia, which is now served by restaurants all around the lake. The fish was surprisingly good.

It was getting late, and it was time for us to return to our missile site. We got on our buses. Everyone was feeling good and talking about all the sites that we visited, the baptismal ceremony, and all the activities that we all participated in at the Town of Jesus.

A week later we were on our way to visit Jerusalem. Our first stop was to the Holocaust Memorial Jewish Museum. The Yad Vashem Museum is Israel's official memorial to the victims of the Holocaust. It is dedicated to preserving the memory of the Jews who were murdered and suffered under the hands of the Nazis. The museum also honored the Jews who fought against their Nazi oppressors and the people who took significant risk to themselves and their families to aid the Jews in need. They also do research of the phenomenon of the Holocaust with the aim of avoiding such event in the future. The Holocaust Museum is more than just a museum; it is a monument to the Holocaust victims and survivors and an educational center. It was a gut-wrenching experience to see what the Jewish people in Europe went through during World War II.

In my God- inspired opinion, this should had been written in the history books as a separate war conducted by the Germans and its allies against the Jewish people. It is believed that up to six million Jews were killed. After seeing these pictures of Auschwitz, Dachau, and other concentration camps; the hall of names of those killed; and photographs, films, documents, letters, works of art, and personal items found in the camps and ghettos, how can anyone in the world question or deny that the Holocaust never happened? ("Yad Vashem: The World Holocaust Remembrance Center, www.yadvashem.org).

We then left the Holocaust Museum and headed to the Israeli parliament building, which is called the Knesset, which means "assembly" in Hebrew. This name recalls the Anshe Knesset, or the Men of the Great Assembly, who convened in Jerusalem during the Second Temple period, to consider and enforce Jewish law, finalize the canonization of the Bible, and institute basic blessings and prayers. Jewish tradition considers these men the final link in the chain of Jewish law giving that began with Moses. While we were in the Knesset, it was said that our secretary of state Cyrus Vance and his team were in this building talking about land for peace. The exchange or return of Palestinian land captured during previous hostilities for peace was considered a part of the war discussion made with Iraq to end the war.

We then visited the Old City to tour the ancient castle ruins of the Tower of David, which has history dating back to the fifth-century CE. The tower was first used in the fifth century CE by the Byzantine Christians, who believed the site to be the palace of King David. I got an unexpected gift when we were shopping, and I found out that the street we were on was the winding street of Via Dolorosa. The Via Dolorosa is a famous tourist attraction because it is the processional route in the Old City of Jerusalem. It represents the path that Jesus would have taken, forced, and beaten by the Roman soldiers on the way to the cross. I am a visual person; so, I tried to visualize the sight and sounds of Jesus, our God, wrapped in the human flesh, gasping for air as he was breathing. His bloody body was struggling with the three-hundred-pound

99

heavy wooden cross upon his shoulder, already weakened by the torture, scourging, humiliations, and the beating that ripped his flesh of his back and legs by the whips, straps, rods, chains, and the cat o' nine tails. He struggled while being beaten by the Roman soldiers and hearing the insults and stones that were being hurled at him by many in the crowd while He was dragging the cross and carrying the sins of the world on his shoulders.

As we walked the Via Dolorosa, I could not stop thinking about Jesus and the pain that He must have endured for us all. Yes, He was God, but God wrapped in a human body that bled and felt pain. I also thought about what it must had been like to be in the crowd, watching helplessly as Jesus was being attacked, abused, and bloodied while passing by. I also thought about how devastated Mary must have felt watching her baby boy being beaten and knowing that He was on His way to the cross and his eventual earthy death. Then I got to thinking about what I know now about that day, what could I have done to help Him, or what would I have done if I was in the crowd? One thing for certain is that I would not have been in the crowd yelling, "Crucify Him," or attempting to throw something at Him.

As we continued to walk the Via Dolorosa, several of the citizens that were there started shouting at us, "Yankees, go home! Yankees, go home!" I believe that some of them were not happy that our secretary of state was in Jerusalem. They were just around the corner from where we were at earlier at the Knesset building talking about the exchange of land for peace. As far as these few citizens that were yelling at us and the leadership of the nation of Israel were concerned, the idea of swapping land for peace was a nonnegotiable subject. The swapping of land for peace never happened even to this day.

It was getting late, and it was time for our trip to end and time for us to return to our missile site. I must admit we all had a wonderful time. I was a little disappointed that we were not able to visit the Western Wall (or the Wailing Wall), the Temple Mount, or the Dome of the Rock. The Western Wall, which is the most religious site in the world for the Jewish people, is located in the Old City of Jerusalem. It is the western support wall of the Temple Mount. Thousands of people journey to the wall every year to visit and recite prayers. When you consider that the Gulf War had just ended, this was not the best time for us to visit these areas anyway, especially since we were all in our military uniforms. All was not totally lost. I did see the Dome of the Rock from looking from the walls of the Tower of David. As a minister, I was blessed by God to have a free education by seeing the historical sites of the Holy Land and learning about them as they came alive to me.

Later that evening, upon our return, we finally got the good news that we have been waiting for. We are scheduled to leave within the next two weeks. I was also told by my platoon leader Lt. Brenda Rivera that I was leaving next week along with several other soldiers that had family emergencies and for those of us that had children born during our war deployment. I immediately called Tammy with the great news. Tammy told the kids that I would be home next week. All I could hear was my children in the background shouting, "Daddy coming home! Daddy coming home!" Of course, I cried with joy hearing the excitement in their young voices that I was coming home soon.

Time to Go Home

I have been in Israel since the day after Iraq launched its first Scud missile attack on January 19, 1991. Today is April 2. The day for to leave Israel had finally arrived. We were all so ready to leave. Since there were no more Scud missiles flying, the citizens of Haifa, Tel Aviv, and Jerusalem were ready for us to leave too. I was excited knowing that I will be seeing my family soon, especially my newborn son, Lloyd Calvin Glover Jr. for the first time. He was born on February 17 during the Gulf War. I had my bags packed, and I was ready to go the day before. I said my goodbyes to my soldiers. We all agreed that we will celebrate our victory over Iraq and have our homecoming celebration next week when everyone else has returned to Germany. I got on the vehicle that took several of us to the air base in Tel Aviv for our departure. It was a beautiful feeling when we arrived at the air base and boarded the plane.

Fifteen minutes after we boarded the plane, the pilot announced over the intercom that our flight would take about four hours before we would touchdown in Germany. He said that we needed to prepare for takeoff. As soon as the plane started to taxi down the runway, I prayed to God for a safe flight home. I could feel the presence of the Holy Spirit as I prayed. He spoke to my spirit that I am a blessed man for my service in protecting His children, for defending the nation of Israel according to His promise that He made to Father Abraham, which is recorded in the first book of the Bible, Genesis 12:3. God Himself said, "I will bless those who bless you and curse those who curse you." I was glad to be on the blessed side of that Bible verse. I cried silently and rejoiced in my seat.

It was a beautiful site looking outside the airplane's window as the plane taxied down the runway and it took off, flying over the beautiful scenery of Tel Aviv. I felt proud knowing that I was a part of the team called the Scud busters that help protect the nation of Israel against the dreaded Iraqi Scud missile attacks and, more importantly, denying Saddam Hussein and his generals their victory, as the Patriot missiles shot down their battle plans to have Israel join the war. Saddam Hussein's objective of dividing the coalition forces was a complete failure, primarily because of us and our prized Patriot missiles. I shouted to myself our Army Air Defense Artillery Command's mottos: "First to Fire" and "If it flies, it dies." "Hoorah" is the Army expression of enthusiasm.

My spirit reminded me that there was a God-ordained reason that God had sent me to Israel as a soldier and an ambassador for Christ. I still was not sure at the time how God wanted to use my experience that I gained in Israel to advance His kingdom. I was like every Christian that prayed the prayer, "God use me for your kingdom and for your glory. And, Lord, send me. I'll go where you want me to go Lord, Amen and Amen." All I knew was that I was a willing vessel and believed that whatever it is that God wanted me to do will be revealed to me in due season or in due time when God wanted me to know.

I was so excited about seeing my family the day before that I barely got any sleep last night. I must have fallen asleep as soon as the plane flew into the clouds. Several hours later, we arrived at the Rhein-Main Air Base in Frankfurt, Germany. I woke up when the pilot announced over the intercom, "Prepare for landing." It felt so good when the plane began its final descent, and I could hear the landing gears opening and the feel of the wheels of the plane touching down on the runway. We all were smiling when the captain announced over the intercom, "Welcome back home to Germany." I was excited and glad to be back to my home away from home.

An hour later, we arrived at the Giessen Army Depot and then to our headquarters' building where Tammy, my kids, and the families of the other soldiers that came back with me were gratefully awaiting our arrival. My eyes started watering as soon as I saw my family. It has been four months since I last saw my wife and kids. I said to myself that my kids had all gotten a little bigger. I got out the vehicle with my hands out so that they could run up to me. My three older kids ran to me, hugged me, and said, "Welcome home, Daddy. We missed you." They all made the cutest welcome home cards that they handed them to me. I quickly read them. They all made me smile. Tammy soon followed with my new gift from God, my newborn son, Lloyd Calvin Glover Jr. Tammy and I kissed and embraced for two minutes. I felt like a victorious battle-hardened soldier returning home to his beautiful queen after four months in a war zone. I was so excited to pick up my newborn son for the first time.

This was the moment that I dreamt about since I was told that he was born. He gave me the biggest baby smile as if he were saying, "Welcome home, Daddy. Nice to meet you too." Our rear detachment captain, Jones, greeted us with a handshake and said with a smile, "Welcome home, Scud busters." He then informed us that we had to go through the returning-home process that included a quick debriefing, completion of paperwork, then we had to turn in our weapons and ammo before we were allowed to leave with our families. The process took less than a half hour. Tammy let me know that she and the kids had prepared me a special meal and that I would have to wait until I got home to find out what it is. I was so excited, and I could not wait to get home to see what the surprise meal that they prepared for me.

Tammy handed me the keys to our vehicle and said, "You drive." It has been four months since the last time that I drove a car. It felt funny at first, but I quickly got the hang of it again. We departed from my unit and headed home. As soon as we arrived home, I drove toward our parking space. I thanked God for me being really back home. Five of my German neighbors that lived in the apartment building that faced our townhouse were outside smoking cigarettes and drinking beer. They were talking and laughing among themselves. They started waving as soon as they saw us pulling in our driveway. They were happy to see me too.

They all came over to our house to welcome me back home. My German neighbors started asking me as they wanted to know what I did in the war. Their eyes lit up when I told them that I was in Israel with a team that used Patriot missiles to shoot down Iraqi Scud missiles. They shook my hand, hugged me, and thank me for us protecting Israel during the war. One of my German friends said, "It's good to have you back." They all agreed, then went back to what they were doing. As soon as I opened the door to our house, all I could smell was fried chicken, collard greens, potato salad, and my favorite, apple pie covered in sugar crumbs. I felt like I was in heaven. We prayed, joked around, and ate that special meal that was prepared for me.

We had a wonderful time celebrating my homecoming. I felt like a king returning home to his castle. I made Tammy a commitment that I will take her out to a restaurant every week to show her my appreciation for her support during the war and for her taking care of my kids while I was deployed. This was a commitment that I have kept to this day. As for my newborn son, I held him in my arms every chance I got because I was not there when he was born.

My newborn son and I

A week later the rest of the unit arrived from Israel. We celebrated the following week with a big barbeque with our families. We were given T-shirts that said our mission was a joint USA-Israel Patriot assignment. We all loved the T-shirts. I was grateful, and I thanked God for keeping His promise that every soldier and family would be safe during our deployment to the Gulf War. All our soldiers that deployed with other units that went to Saudi Arabia, Iraq, or Kuwait, including Specialist Mims, returned to our unit within the following two weeks as well. We were all glad to see him.

We celebrated his return. We all wanted to know what he did, where he was, and what Patriot unit that he was assigned to during the war. He said that he was in Saudi Arabia with a task force 8/43 ADA, a Patriot battalion from Fort Bliss. He said that the battalion went as far as forty miles from Bagdad, and he had surprisingly good war

stories that he shared with us as well. We shared our war experiences with him too. He was really impressed but not surprised when we told him that we shot down every Scud missile that Iraq fired at the Haifa area.

106

Haifa Patriot shirt

It was good being back in Germany. The only thing that we did not have was a returning home ceremony and parade. We never did have any type of welcome-home ceremony or parade like our servicemen and women received back in the States. That was one of my disappointments about being deployed to a war zone from a foreign country. I am assuming that the thought must have never occurred to the leadership of the Giessen military command to have one big ceremony in celebration for all the combat and support units that was from the Giessen depot that participated in the war. All that was important was that we were safe and back home in Germany with our families and our friends.

On my first weekend back, I went for a run. As soon as the cows saw me, they started mooing, the chickens started plucking, the roosters started cock-a-doodle-doing, and the sheep started baaing. It was funny, but I took it as a gesture that they all missed me and were glad that I was back. I started waving at them and laughing. I shouted at them, "I missed you all too!" My spirit told me that they were saying to each other that the Jesus man is back. I started shouting in tongues into the atmosphere and thanking God that I was back too.

Returning to our church family and to our Sunday services and our midweek Bible studies was great too. Staff Sergeant (Pastor) George Gadson along with Sergeant (Minister) Glen Murchison were both deployed to Israel with me. Staff Sergeant Gadson and I were stationed in Haifa while Sergeant Murchison was stationed in Tel Aviv during the war. Several other ministers and church brothers and sisters from our church that were also deployed with their units to the war started returning to Giessen Army Depot and to our church family as well. We celebrated and thanked God that we did not lose anyone in the war. Pastor Gadson preached a magnificent welcome-home service. As a minister, it felt good sitting back in the pulpit with my fellow brothers in ministry.

A month after our return, our church was selected to host a three-day revival that included several other churches from around the Giessen and Frankfurt area. The revival was scheduled for next month. Being that our church was the host church, Pastor Gadson wanted all the ministers to have black suits. The request was nice, but the problem was that most of us did not have a black suit at the time with us in Germany. What made matters worse, the PX store (short for Army Post Exchange), which is our primary store for shopping, did not have any available black suits that any of us could fit, nor did any of the surrounding German stores have black suits. Several of the ministers had to travel to several separate locations around Germany (within a fifty-mile radius) to find black suits. I was scheduled that weekend for senior sergeant duty, so I could not travel with them.

So, I took the chance and went to our Giessen Depot's thrift shop for the first time. I prayed that I would find one that I could fit. It was miraculous when I asked the store clerk if they had a black suit. She told me with a smile that she had just put one on the rack less than a minute ago that looked like I could fit. She took me where it was on the rack. The suit was new, or it looked like it was worn just one

108

time. It had a surprisingly decent price of thirty dollars, and get this, it was a perfect fit with the right size that I needed. I thanked God. I shouted in the store God's name, "Jehovah-Jireh, the Lord will provide." The people shopping in the thrift shop looked around to see what was going on. I just smiled. When they saw me carrying the suit, they got the message. I knew that this was no one but God's work. This was my-ram-in-the-bush moment. I praised the Lord, knowing that he was the provider of this suit.

The revival was great, and we all had a blessed time. There was one funny, but an awkward, moment during the revival for me when the church superintendent's wife tried to preach a sermon by verbatim (minus the military parts) of a well-known sermon that was preached by my idol, the evangelist R. W. Schambach. This was a sermon I had on tape, that I loved, and that I would listen to all the time. The sermon was "Power over the Devil." I was not sure if I was the only one that noticed this, but knowing this made her sermon rendition sound flat. I learned a valuable preaching lesson from this: that you should never ever try to preach someone else's sermon without having that preachers anointing. Amen.

It was early August 1991 when we received the words that our unit was placed on a one-year rotation to Saudi Arabia to replace a Patriot missile battalion that was there from Fort Bliss, Texas. Our new orders had us scheduled to deploy for another combat tour, this time to the Kingdom of Saudi Arabia with an arrival date sometime in February 1992. Even though the war was technically over, Saddam Hussein was still in power, still a menace to this region of the Middle East and was still the murderous dictator of the Iraqi people. He still had those hidden Scud missiles and other weapons of mass destruction that he did not want the coalition forces to discover. This time, unlike our previous deployment to Israel during the Gulf War, we had six months to prepare.

In September 1992, I got a blessing of a lifetime. This was from no one but God. This was proof that God is the Author and Finisher of my faith. He stepped in and ordered my next steps. Our current battalion reenlistment noncommission officer (NCO) Sergeant First Class Bailey received orders to return to the United States to attend the Army's first sergeant's leadership course at Fort Bliss. He asked me if I was interested in replacing him because of my prior experience as an Army recruiter. Of course, I said yes. I accepted the assignment as the new battalion reenlistment noncommission officer. Talking to our soldiers was something that I was good it. I quickly learned the job. My primary responsibility was to reenlist or convince good soldiers to stay in the Army for more years. I felt honored every time when one of our soldiers agreed to reenlist based on the information that I provided to them. This gave each soldier the opportunity to serve more time defending our great country. Some of our soldiers received reenlistment bonuses and others reenlisted for new jobs and others reenlisted for their choice of duty stations. I took pride in that I was keeping our Army strong by reenlisting the best soldiers in the Army. Hoorah!

Ministering in Saudi Arabia

I could not help but to think about our first deployment to Israel during the Gulf War. My unit deployed from Germany to the nation of Israel as part of the joint task force Patriot missiles in defense of the nation of Israel. Our mission then was to protect Israel against Saddam Hussein's Iraqi Scud missile attacks. I was the platoon sergeant over our fire control platoon then. A year later, this time I was going over to Saudi Arabia in a different role as the battalion's reenlistment noncommission officer. As a platoon sergeant, I had a leadership role in a combat environment. This time I have a support role. Both roles are just as important in the success of our mission. Our unit's mission this time was to protect the Kingdom of Saudi Arabia from the same potential Scud missile attacks from Iraq.

Even though Israel and Saudi Arabia are common enemies, the truth is that, both the Muslims and Arabs (who for the most part are Islamic) and the Jews, along with the Christians, are all Abrahamic religions, which worship the God of Abraham. Abraham, who is called Ibrahim in the Qur'an, is the same Father Abraham that is in the Christian Bible, the Islamic Qur'an, and in the Jewish Torah (also called the Laws, or the five books of Moses). Father Abraham had to two sons, Ishmael and Isaac. Father Abraham's firstborn son, Ishmael, was born by his handmaiden Hagar. It is believed that many Muslims and Arabs are descendants of Ishmael. Abraham's second son was Isaac, who was born to Abraham's wife, Sarah. The Israelis are descendants of his promised son, Isaac, by his wife Sarah. There has always been a conflict in the Middle East through time about who is Abraham's promised son. I challenge you to read Genesis 16–18:1–15 and 21:1–21 to fully understand the full story.

On February 20, our missile battalion deployed to the Kingdom of Saudi Arabia for a four-month tour. We were assigned to the King Khalid Military Center. Upon our arrival, it was hot and dry. The temperature was easily above 105 degrees. There were sand dunes everywhere. It was amazing seeing the wild and domesticated camels walking in herds in the distance under the Saudi sun. The camel is the national animal of Saudi Arabia. They even have camel beauty pageants. The good thing about being in Saudi Arabia was the fact that there were no Scud missiles flying. We still had to be prepared just in case Saddam Hussein decided to end the peace agreement by firing Scud missiles again.

It was nice staying in air- conditioned barracks and not in tents like so many of our soldiers had to do in Israel. I had my own barrack room in another building, away from the lower-ranked soldiers because I was a senior sergeant. Being that I was the battalion reenlistment sergeant, I had my own office as well. The Saudi military center was nice. We had a beautiful dining facility that served great meals. There was also a chapel that we could attend church services there. The only problem when we first got there was that we did not have an Army chaplain.

God was good. About a week later, several of us soon learned that there was a church service that was being conducted twenty miles away at the Eskan Village Air Force Base in Riyadh. Somehow, we got permission for four of us to attend these services. Every Sunday the four of us (me, Sergeant First Class Vincent Kennedy, Staff Sergeant Contee, and Sergeant Glenn Murchison) would load up in a Suburban wagon and travel the twenty miles to attend the church services at the Air Force base. I coined us the Faithful Four. We would sing gospel songs and joke a lot on the way. We had church prior to arriving at our destination. The Eskan village services were conducted under the supervision of their Air Force chaplain; however, the services were conducted by several Air Force airmen that were also ministers from their home churches in the United States. Pastor Philleas A. Hill, an airmen, was the pastor. Every service was a spirit-filled service. We praised and worshipped the Lord together. We all had great times, and we made several new friends. All of us were well liked by our Air Force brothers and sisters that attended these services with us.

The Faithful Four

The Army sent us a chaplain, Captain Reed, who arrived a week later. All the brothers and sisters that believed in Christ celebrated his arrival. Chaplain Reed was also a Methodist seminary-trained chaplain just like Captain Dugal, who was the chaplain during our deployment to Israel. Chaplain Reed was well liked and received by the soldiers of our unit. The four of us were already committed to our Eskan Village service, but some of us did attend his midweek Bible study. Chaplain Reed also conducted an inspirational Sunday church service. A lot of our brothers and sisters did attend his services. I learned a lot about ministering from Chaplain Reed. My church upbringing was nondenominational, but more in line with Church of God in Christ-type of service and speaking in tongues. Chaplain Reed's services were more aligned with traditional Methodist teaching. I loved Chaplain Reed and was grateful for everything I learned from him from our Bible study classes, but I was hungry and was more interested in a more spiritual tongue-speaking service.

Being in Saudi and being assigned as the reenlistment sergeant was a blessing from God for me. It gave me plenty of time, when I was not soldiering, to study the Bible and study the Christian resources that I bought with me. I would also minister the gospel to fellow soldiers when they had the available time and or when they had questions about the Bible. I was also known as the sergeant that had all the good gospel music. I bought a collection of gospel music cassette tapes and Bible lessons with me to listen during my evening times. I collected most of my music from Minister (Sergeant) Murchison in preparation for our deployment. I had a collection of cassette tapes that I would share with anyone who asked.

I made it a point to call Tammy twice a week to speak with her and the kids. A quick prayer for our safety was a major part of our calls. To pass the time away in the evenings, about five of us would run up to five to seven miles in one way and run back on the Saudi roads that was outside our compound. We had to wait until the evening, which was the coolest part of the day. On many of those days, I chose to run by myself so that I could spend private time alone with God. I would always pray for my safety first and ask God to put a hedge of protection around me as I ran. Every time I would speak and listen for his voice to speak to my spirit. I could feel His presence as I ran. I quickly learned by the unction of the Holy Spirit that the same God that spoke to me and was present while I ran in New Jersey, Philadelphia, Ohio, Texas, Germany, and in Israel is the same God that spoke to me and was present with me when I ran on the roads of Saudi Arabia. He is certainly the same God no matter where I ran. The spiritual truth is that God is omnipresent, meaning He is everywhere. He is the same God of Father Abraham, Isaac, Ishmael, Jacob—and, yes, let me add, little o' me. Amen and Amen.

I would also listen to my gospel music, preaching sermon, or a Bible-study tape as I ran. I made it a daily practice and a learning tool for me to recite aloud into the atmosphere on what I just learned from these tapes. The open air and open road were my preaching and teaching practice grounds. I took pleasure in shouting out the name of Jesus and the names of God. I would practice two different names of God and there meaning each day that I ran as a part of my learning. I would say God is Elohim (He is your Creator), God is Elohim Chayim (He is the Living God), God is Abba (He is your Father), God is Jehovah-Jireh (the Lord will provide), God is Jehovah-shalom (the Lord is Peace), God is El Elyon (He is your Sovereign), God is El Kanna (The Jealous God), God is El Roi (He sees you). God is Jehovah Ro'I (He is your Shepherd), and God is Jehovah Nissi (He is my banner).

God gave me an assignment to plant seeds into the Saudi atmosphere with the Gospel truth that Jesus Christ was the Son of God, the Lord of lords, and the Savior of the world. I would speak with God and pray that my words would bounce around the atmosphere and would drop in the hearing of a Saudi or other citizen from other counties that was living or working in the nearby towns and villages from our missile site. I was standing on Isaiah 55:11, which says, "So is my word that goes out from my mouth: It will not return to me empty but will accomplish what I desire and achieve the purpose for which I sent it."

The truth is that I felt when I was running that there was nobody on these roads that was paying me any attention. It seemed like the fathers or male Saudi citizens that were driving on these roads were speeding up and down these roads with their wives, female relatives, and children sitting in the back seats and were more focused on looking religious according to Saudi customs. As much as I wanted to, I could not wave or make any friendly gesture to them because we were told by an Army captain during our initial Saudi's custom briefing not to do this because it could have the potential of them misunderstand o u r intentions or our normal way of saying something. I did not want to take the chance by waving especially since I was out there running by myself. There were on several occasions that I saw camels with their shepherds wandering close to where I was running in the desert. I would spoke in the atmosphere that Jesus is Lord hoping that the camels would hear me and would say something to their shepherds. My spirit reminded me that God once used a donkey (Num. 22:28) to speak to Balaam. I thought with a smile that right now would be a suitable time for God to do the same.

There were days when I would spend time talking with Chaplain Reed in the chapel about me going to seminary or a Bible college once I retired from the Army. He thought it was a surprisingly promising idea. He also liked my plans for what I was planning to do once we returned to Germany. Chaplain Reed and I hit it off fairly good. He also understood that he was a Methodist chaplain and that several of us that attended the service at Eskan Village were more in line with a Church of God in Christ type of service and that we had a spiritual need to be in a church service that we were more accustomed to. I could tell that Chaplain Reed was not offended by our discussion about us attending another church service away from where we were at this base. It came as no surprise to me that he was not disappointed by us attending the service at Eskan village. It was a matter of fact; he encouraged us to attend the services of our choosing.

Being that I was the battalion's reenlistment sergeant, I had the opportunity to collaborate closely with him because many of our Christian brothers and sisters that were eligible to reenlist wanted Chaplain Reed to be the officer that gave them their reenlistment oath. I am honored to say that Sergeant Murchison and I were two of those soldiers that reenlisted while we were in Saudi Arabia by Captain Reed.

Sergeant Murchison's reenlistment ceremony

After Sergeant Murchison's reenlistment ceremonies, Chaplain Reed asked me if I would be interested in volunteering to be his driver. He needed someone to go along with him to visit different American government sites to assist him in conducting church services. Of course, I said yes, and I jumped at this opportunity to do something special for God's kingdom. I felt the power of the Holy Spirit. I knew then, just like I knew back in Israel, that there was something that God wanted me to see, to do, or to be a part of something great for His kingdom and for His glory. Amen.

I answered the call and volunteered to travel alongside our Army chaplain as part of God's Army to assist him in conducting church services at isolated United States government compounds and communication sites. Chaplain Reed explained to me that because of an agreement between our governments, our government sites could not have their own chaplains officially assigned to these locations. This is because of Saudi's customs. We had an enjoyable time conducting these services. The government employees and their family members at these locations were happy to see us. Each time we conducted a service, they would verbally communicate to us how much they appreciated us coming out to their locations. After we conducted our first service at a communications site, we were asked to go to another room where there was a few Saudis and two citizens from other countries that wanted to know more about the Gospel. We were surprised but happy to minister to them. This was a golden opportunity and a setup by God for us to be here. They came to us because they were willing to hear more about the Good News. You could feel and see in their eyes that they had a zeal for God and a hunger for more information about Jesus Christ. Word soon got out to the other locations, and we were able to minister at three other locations.

Trusting God to Orchestrate the Opportunity

Chaplain Reed and I believed in our hearts that God had orchestrated the opportunities for us to safely conduct these

services. Never in my wildest dream would I have ever envisioned that one day that I would be ministering and conducting services in Saudi Arabia, in all places in the world, but to minister to Saudi citizens and migrant workers from other countries on Saudi soil. Conducting Christian services on any non-Christian country is termed an underground Christian church service, which is forbidden in most, if not all, Arab countries, especially in the Kingdom of Saudi Arabia. We knew the risk and counted it joy trusting by faith that God had our backs and that His Spirit was with us.

We stood on the written words of the following verses:

> For the Spirit God gave us does not make us timid but gives us power, love, and self-discipline. (2 Tim. 1:7)

> The Great Commission: And Jesus came and said to them, "All authority in heaven and on earth has been given to me. Go therefore and make disciples of all nations, baptizing them in the name of the Father and of the Son and of the Holy Spirit, and teaching them to observe all that I have commanded you. And behold, I am with you always, to the end of the age." (Matt. 28:18–20)

> But you will receive power when the Holy Spirit comes on you; and you will be my

119

witnesses in Jerusalem, and in all Judea and Samaria, and to the ends of the earth. (Acts 1:8)

I can do all this through him who gives me strength. (Phil. 4:13)

"No weapon forged against you will prevail, and you will refute every tongue that accuses you. This is the heritage of the servants of the Lord, and this is their vindication from me," declares the Lord. (Isaiah 54:17)

Let me give some example of the danger and trouble with which we were faced. Our Army chaplain, Captain Reed, had to remove his chaplain's cross insignia off his hat and also had to cover his chaplain's branch insignia on his collar prior to us leaving our missile site. Any Christian materials such as Bibles and any other Christian literatures that we were carrying had to be well hidden until we arrived at our destinations. Saudi authorities had the legal power to confiscate and destroy these materials if discovered. This thoughts of the danger and trouble that we could had been in never crossed our minds at the time; but the most dangerous part of this was, if our activities were discovered by the Saudis, we would have been reported to their religious authority and our Army chain of command. It would have been up to our Army command to take some course of action to discipline us. The truth is, we put our safety in the hands of the Holy Spirit to put a hedge of protection over our lives. Amen.

Sadly, after about six weeks of us conducting these services, Chaplain Reed became ill with an unknown disease. He left suddenly one day because he had to be transferred back to the United States for medical treatment that he desperately needed and could not get in Saudi Arabia. I was hurt when I found out that the chaplain had left. I was not an Army chaplain, so I could not conduct these services on my own during Chaplain Reed's absence. We all were hoping and praying that he would have a speedy recovery and that he would return soon. Later, we were told that he had developed leukemia, and he was not coming back. I was sad when I heard the news that he was not returning because I did not have the opportunity to say goodbye and to thank him for the experience and the friendship that I gained from working alongside of him. It was an honor and a blessing to know and to serve with Chaplain Reed. I know that God had put him on my path of life for me to grow spiritually from his experience. A year later, after our return to Germany, we heard he had passed away. We were all sad to hear the news of his passing. I prayed for his family, and I thank God for Chaplain Reed and the relationship that I had with him. I am still praying that this information was not true. Amen.

It took a month before another Army chaplain arrived. Our new chaplain was not as friendly or as outgoing as Chaplain Reed. I never did establish a good relationship with our new chaplain like I did with Chaplain Reed. It could have been because I was committed to our services that I attended at Eskan Village Air Force Base in Riyadh. I did discuss with our new chaplain about what Chaplain Reed and I had accomplished ministering at those government sites and the underground churches. He said he would consider it. Being that he was new, he did not have the connections that Chaplain Reed had. He never did get back to me. I often thought about those brothers and sisters that we did minister to at those government sites. As much as I wanted to go back and finish ministering, I could not without the new Army chaplain. I was glad and grateful for the times that Chaplain Reed and I had spent together ministering at these locations. It was a blessing that we added to their understanding and love of Jesus Christ. We did leave Bibles and other Bible study materials with them each time during our visits. My prayer is that someone there would have stepped up and filled in the gap and continued the services that Chaplain Reed started. Amen.

On April 12, at the end of our church service at Eskan Village, we were all presented with certificates of appreciation. We were surprised when Pastor Hill called us up to the front of the church. They had accidently presented these to us because they thought that we were leaving Saudi Arabia the following week. The certificates were nice. They were signed by our pastor Philleas A. Hill, who was in the Air Force. The certificate read, "For outstanding service to the Gospel Ministry at Eskan Village." They wanted to recognize us and to show their appreciation for us taking the time to travel those twenty miles each Sunday mornings and our Spirit-filled contribution to their church services. Pastor Hill wanted to personally thank each one of us for contributing to their services. We all laugh when he was informed by us that he will be stuck will us until June. He was embarrassed by the certificate presentation, but happy to know that we still had more time together to praise the Lord. Amen.

Eskan Village certificate

122

One day in May, I was given an assignment to travel with a supply room soldier to our Air Force base in Dhahran to exchange and pick up a new vehicle and other military equipment for our unit. Dhahran was the same place last year where twenty-four of our Army reserved soldier were killed from a Scud missile attack. While I was there, I was talking to an Air Force brother that was processing our equipment request. This led to a beautiful conversation about Christ. He said he was a Christian and could easily tell that I was a Christian too. To my surprise, we were both ministers. He told me that there was a planned revival that weekend at the Khobar Tower Complex on the Dhahran Air Force base. He was one of the revival planners. He asked me if I wanted to attend. My response was yes, but I would need a supernatural intervention by God because of the short notice, that it was an overnight event, and the distance I would need to travel. The brother looked at me and boldly said, "Is there anything too hard for our God?" We did a quick prayer for God to step in and open doors so that I could attend. We touched and agreed and declared it was done in Jesus's name. Amen.

He gave me a contact name and phone number that I could call to plan my attendance. He also said that I could stay in their visiting noncommission officer's guest dormitory. I thanked the brother for the information and the prayer. I made a promise in faith that I would be back to attend the revival. I thought that it was only God that put this brother in my path so that I could find out about this revival. God gave me this assignment because He had something great that He wanted me to see and something that He wanted me to experience and share with the world about how the servicemen and servicewomen of the Air Force conducted a spiritual revival on Saudi soil. Amen.

When I return to my missile site, I had to get permission from my chain of command to return to Dhahran for the weekend. Permission was easily given to me. I called the contact number that the brother gave me. I was given permission to stay in the noncommission officer's visitor's dormitory. I packed up my bag, and I headed out that Friday afternoon for the weekend. I traveled the sixty miles back to Dhahran by myself. I must have cried, sang, and prayed to God the whole time during my drive. I arrived and was given a beautiful room in the NCO visitor's dormitory. The Dhahran revival was scheduled for Saturday and Sunday. I could only attend the Saturday evening service because I had to be back to our base by Sunday afternoon. The revival was great and powerful.

There were at least two hundred or more servicemen and servicewomen in attendance at this service, worshipping and praising God. We sang, danced, and listened to some great preaching being delivered by my fellow Air Force ministers. It was great being back in a service where so many brothers and sisters were speaking and singing in the spirit. This was the greatest move of God that I have ever participated in even to this day. And yes, I have participated in many great moves of God before and after that revival in Saudi Arabia. They were great moves of God too, but none like this.

My spiritual relationship with God was elevated several levels during and after the service. My life and the love for God were changed forever. I did see the brother that gave me the information about the revival from a distance. I did not get the opportunity to thank him because he was one of the main preachers that spoke at this event. Just in case you missed this—this move of God and this revival happened on the soil of Saudi Arabia. I returned to my room after the revival was over. I lay in my bed rejoicing and crying that God had orchestrated this revival and that He gave little old me the divine privilege to attend this move of God in the land of Saudi Arabia. Hallelujah! I got up that Sunday morning and began my journey back to our missile site. I felt the presence of the Holy Spirit that was with me the whole time on my way back. The Holy Spirit whispered to my spirit to record this event in my prayer journal. I rolled down my windows in this vehicle, and I sang and shouted "Hallelujah" out the window until I arrived back to our missile site.

Our unit is scheduled to return to Germany in a week. We had one more Sunday left in Saudi Arabia. The four of us, who I called the Faithful Four, were sad, along with our Eskan church family, when the day came for us to attend our last church service with them. They gave us a going-away party and thanked us again for our contribution to their service. I mentioned earlier that they accidently presented us all certificates of appreciation back on April 12 because they thought that we were leaving Saudi Arabia then. We joked and laughed about this, but this time we were really leaving. We hugged our Air Force brother and sisters, and we prayed together and said our final goodbyes. On June 30, we left Saudi Arabia, heading back to Germany.

What I Learned Being in Saudi Arabia

On July 30, my entire battalion of Patriot soldiers were sitting on planes on a Saudi airstrip, awaiting our turn to take off for our return flight back to Germany. We were celebrating the end of this tour. This day was special to me too because this was my tenth wedding anniversary. Tammy and I have been married since July 30, 1982, and I was on my way home to celebrate this special day too. As the plane that I was on started to taxi down the runway, I prayed for our safety, which has been my spiritual duty before each flight. I started having flashbacks about last year around this same time that I was on a returning flight from Israel to Germany after what we thought was the end of the Gulf War. I was tired back then on this flight because I did not get any sleep the night before because I was so excited that I was going to see my family and especially my newborn son for the first time. He was born during the war on February 17, 1991.

Even though that was a year ago, I was still restless and excited to get back to Germany and to see my family this time around. Tammy and the kids were happy that I was coming home too. They were more relaxed than I was. Tammy by now was a seasoned Army wife who had mastered the survival skills and had wartime experience as a soldier's spouse from my last combat tour to the Gulf War. She had no problems during my absence, and she did a fantastic job of providing for my family and taking care of all our family affairs without me being present. My son, who was born during the war, was a year older now and was now walking. Besides that, I did get enough sleep last night as compared to a year ago.

The flight from Saudi Arabia was 2,679 miles away and a little over six hours in flight time. We had six hours before our plane would land in Germany. This gave me plenty of time to reminisce about my life during these past two years and think about how my life changed because of one man's decision to conduct an invasion of the sovereign emirate of Kuwait back in the summer of July 1990. Saddam Hussein's decision caused my unit to spend combat tours in both Israel and Saudi Arabia. His decision also cost me valuable time with my family as well, especially those moments that can't be replaced: me seeing my kids growing up during those months that I was away.

I did miss my family during these deployments. As a soldier, I understood the sacrifices of going to war and the cost of freedom. This was a sacrifice that I was willing to pay for the safety and security of my family. I also understood that there are lifetime benefits that comes with serving in the military and going to war. Tammy, my kids, my family back in New Jersey, and all of America considered me a war hero. I can now say with pride that I am a veteran of the Gulf War, and I can join the local chapter of the Veterans of Foreign Wars (VFW) after my retirement from the Army.

I am sure that none of my fellow soldiers would agree with me on this, but spiritually speaking, I counted both tours as a blessing for me. It took me years to realize how great this time was for my ministry. I want to take this time to look back and remember what exactly God gave to me to see and to do during these two years. Most importantly, God gave me the priceless opportunity to soldier in the defense of the nation of Israel and a year later to serve in the defense of the Kingdom of Saudi Arabia. I felt blessed, and I felt the favor of God over my life knowing that there are few, if not any other, ministers, except for the possibility of Sergeant Glenn Murchison, in the world that can say they spend time ministering as a soldier and as an ambassador for Christ in both Saudi Arabia and Israel. Defending Israel was a blessing to all of us watchmen who protected the skies of Israel against the Scud missile attacks. God Himself did say to Father Abraham in Genesis 12:3, "I will bless those who bless you, and whoever curses you I will curse and all peoples on earth will be blessed through you." This blessing applied to all of us that were Patriot defenders in Israel. Amen.

I am blessed by this revelation from the Holy Spirit, and I have claimed this blessing (Gen. 12:3) ever since the day that I got on the plane, leaving for Israel, last year. God also gave me the opportunity to walk among the Jewish people in the cities and sites in Israel like Haifa (Mount Carmel in the Bible; the Sea of Galilee; Tel Aviv; Capernaum, which is called the Town of Jesus) and Jerusalem (where we visited the Jewish capitol building, the Knesset; Holocaust Memorial Museum; and the remnants of the Second Temple). We also had the opportunity to visit where Jesus conducted the Sermon of the Mount (the Beatitudes). For us soldiers, we had a rare opportunity to be baptized in the Sea of Galilee by Chaplain Dugal and Pastor Gadson.

As a minister, I was blessed to get a free education by seeing and learning firsthand about the historical sites in the Holy Land, which came alive to me. There is no Bible college, seminary, or an online course that could have given me the opportunity and experience to see or serve in Israel. It was only God who orchestrated this precious time for me. God turned a war situation into a learning workshop for me. Visiting these locations were priceless. Therefore, I am sharing my story on why God has called me to share the Good News.

I also learned from my service in Saudi Arabia as well. We did have the opportunity to walk and shop among the great people of Saudi Arabia. The Saudis were gracious and welcoming to us. I found Saudi Arabia to be more religious than Israel, especially when it came down to their hours of prayer and their religious laws. It was interesting the first time that we heard the Islamic call to worship. All the Saudis and Islamic migrant workers from other countries all started kneeling on prayer rugs and praying toward the direction of Mecca while others went to the local mosque to pray. I found Sharia law and the treatment of their women troubling and living in the past. Saudi Arabia still has the Al-Safaa Square, which is also known to the world as Chop-Chop Square. The Saudis also calls it Justice Square. This is a historical landmark in Riyadh where they still punish criminals by cutting off their heads, hands, and feet, depending on the nature of the crime that their citizen had committed and found guilty by Sharia law. We were told by a Saudi that at any given time an unannounced execution could happen. The Saudi police and other officials would show up to clear the square to make way for an execution to take place ("Deera Square," *Wikipedia*). Half of our soldiers were interested in seeing the site and wanted to visit the square to see if this would really happen.

One day five of us were out shopping at a Saudi market in Riyadh. We heard that the Al-Safa Square was nearby, so we decided to drive by the square just to see what it looked like and to see if something was going on at the square. It was an eerie feeling as we drove by. I was glad that there was no activity that was going on in the square that day. On our way back to the base, we noticed that there were about eleven poor and destitute Saudi or migrant women wailing on the side of the road begging for help. They were covered in their black Islamic abaya from head to toes. It was like something that you could read out of the Bible about people begging for alms. We felt sorry for them, but there was nothing that we could have done to help them or give them money because we were not sure if this violated some type of Saudi custom or one of their cultural rules.

We did attend church services and Bible studies on our missile base. Four of us would travel from our base every Sunday to attend services with our Air Force brothers and sisters at their air base in Riyadh. We had great times together worshipping God. I have to say that the two greatest moments for me as a believer of Christ during these two years was when I visited Capernaum, the Sea of Galilee, and Jerusalem and when God stepped in and made the arrangements for me to participate in the Dhahran revival that happen on Saudi soil. My spiritual relationship with God was elevated to a higher level during and after the revival. My life and the love for God changed forever. Amen. My greatest moments as a soldier happened when I found out that my son was born and when President Bush announced that the Gulf War was over.

Soldiering in both Israel and Saudi Arabia taught me a valuable lesson about the seeds of Father Abraham. I learned that even in war, the Christians, Muslims, and Jews are all brothers and sisters, regardless of religious preference because of our love and inheritance from Father Abraham. We are all God's creation, and we all believe and benefit from God's promises to Father Abraham. The Bible says that Father Abraham's first two sons were Ishmael and Isaac. Ishmael being Father Abraham's firstborn son. I can still remember singing the song about Father Abraham as a little kid when my family attended the Lutheran church. The song's lyrics went like this:

Father Abraham had many sons. Many sons had Father Abraham. I am one of them and so are you. So, let's all praise the Lord.

It is hard to believe that so many people around the world do not understand or accept the fact that we are all considered a part of the Abrahamic religions: the Christians, Muslims, and Jews.

You will have to read along with me Genesis 17:15–21 to fully understand what happened during this time and how God had blessed both sons and their everlasting connection. Let's read it together.

God also said to Abraham, "As for Sara your wife, you are no longer to call her Sarai; her name will be Sarah. I will bless her and will surely give you a son by her. I will bless her so that she will be the mother of nations; kings of peoples will come from her." Abraham fell facedown; he laughed and said to himself, "Will a son be born to a man a hundred years old? Will Sarah bear a child at the age of ninety?" And Abraham said to God, "If only Ishmael might live under your blessing!" Then God said, "Yes, but your wife Sarah will bear you a son, and you will call him Isaac. I will establish my covenant with him as an everlasting covenant for his descendants after him. and as for Ishmael, I have heard you: I will surely bless him; I will make him fruitful and will increase his numbers. He will be the father of twelve rulers, and I will make him into a great nation. but my covenant I will establish with Isaac, whom Sarah will bear to you by this time next year."

I am not trying to make a political statement, but I felt during the war that the root cause of most of the conflict between Jews, Christians, and Muslims have to do with one's interpretations of the promises that God made to Father Abraham about who is the blessed or the promised son. The Jews and Christians believe it was Isaac, while the Muslims believe it was given to Ishmael because he was the firstborn to Father Abraham by his hand servant Hagar. Genesis 16:15–16 says, "So, Hagar bore Abram a son, and Abram gave the name Ishmael to the son she had borne. Abram was eighty-six years old when Hagar bore him Ishmael." The Bible says that Ishmael was born of the flesh, while Isaac was born of the spirit.

We soon arrived back to Germany. It took us a little while to get our equipment off the planes. We were all glad to be back in Germany and with our families. It was a joy seeing my family again after our second deployment in Saudi Arabia. Upon our return from Saudi Arabia, the military was going through a major downsizing of its active duty forces that was built up in preparation for the Gulf War. It has been two years since the beginning of the buildup of troops in preparation for the Gulf War, and it was time to reduce the number of active duty soldiers in the Army. The downsizing allowed eligible soldiers the opportunity to leave the Army earlier before their enlistment or reenlistment contracts were up.

The downsizing also allowed soldiers that had more than fifteen years of active military service the opportunity to retire early with partial retirement benefits. I had sixteen years invested in the Army, a growing family to take care of, and four years left for full retirement. I chose to remain in the Army to complete my twenty years of service. I also had orders that had us departing Germany for Fort Bliss in three weeks on August 21, 1992. This really did not give us enough time to pack up our furniture, sell my German car, and fully process out of Germany. I also had three weeks to serve our church family and say my final goodbyes. I was overcome with joy when I was presented with a letter of good standing from Pastor Gadson and an award plaque presented to me by all the ministers in appreciation for my service as a minister at this church.

Back in Good Old USA

On August 21, 1992, my family and I departed Frankfurt, Germany, on a military airlift command flight to the United States. It was a peaceful flight in the beginning until my youngest son, Lloyd Calvin Jr., who was two years old at the time, started crying several hours into the flight. He, along with other small kids, must have cried during most of the flight. Whenever he was not asleep, my son would cry. I did not feel so bad during the flight because of his crying. There were other small kids on the flight that were crying just as much as he did. Some of them were crying more loudly then my son. The flight took a little over eight hours, which seem felt like it took forever. Our flight finally landed in LaGuardia, Airport in Queens, New York.

Everyone on the plane was relieved when we landed in New York, not only because of our kids crying, but because of the length of the flight. It felt so good being back in the good old USA. Some of the soldiers and their family members were actually crying when the pilot announced, "Welcome to the United States of America. The weather is 82 degrees and sunny in Queens, New York." I shouted, "Hallelujah," and praised the Lord for a safe flight home. I got out the plane and yelled, "Thank you, Jesus!" I was not alone because other soldiers and some of their family members followed my lead, saying "Thank you, Jesus" too. It has been three years since most of us were last in the United States.

I was born and raised in New Jersey, and my wife, Tammy, was born and raised in Cleveland, Ohio. The same city that we first met and fell in love back in the 1980s. We had twenty-eight days to visit our families in New Jersey and Cleveland. The Army allowed me three additional days for travel time before I had to report to Fort Bliss.

We spent the first fifteen days in New Jersey. I purchased a used 1986 Chevrolet sedan for a thousand dollars in cash to get us by until we arrive in El Paso. The owner who happened to be present at the time was asking for two thousand dollars. I told him that I was a soldier that just returned from Germany traveling with my family to Fort Bliss, Texas. I told him the truth that I really needed a car and that I only had a thousand dollars to spare.

He thought about it for a moment, called his wife, came back, and agreed to my offer. He said that God told him to sell it to me for a thousand dollars. We shook hand. He gave me the title and keys. He thanked me for my service before he hugged me goodbye. This was my second ram-in-the-bush moment. We had a wonderful time visiting my family during our nine days in New Jersey. We celebrated by having barbeques and fish fries while we were there. We had families that came from New York and Georgia to help us celebrate while we were in New Jersey.

I made it a point to visit my father and Sister Linda's grave site. This was the first time that I could visit them because I was in Germany these past three years. Two days before we departed for Cleveland, a Christian brother Randolph Hunter, who was a family friend, came by. We had a friendly conversation about Jesus. We finished our talk with a prayer fest in my mother's front yard. As we prayed, we could spiritually feel strongholds and generational curses being broken and healings being dispatched throughout Plainfield. Two days later we departed for Cleveland to spend the next eight days there. Tammy's family were excited when we arrived in Cleveland too. We had families from Cleveland and Columbus that came and helped us celebrate our homecoming while we were in Cleveland.

It was great seeing and being with our families and close friends during each of these visits. I did attend church services and Bible studies each Sunday and Wednesdays while I was there. They were Church in God in Christ services in New Jersey. I did acknowledge the Father, Son, and Holy Spirit during the visitor's welcome. The church members gave me a standing ovation when I mentioned that I was a soldier and an ambassador for Christ, detailing my service in the Gulf War, protecting both Israel and Saudi Arabia against Scud missile attacks. I did attend services at the New Life Independent Ministries Church that I was a member and licensed a minister while I lived in Cleveland. Pastor Lewis was happy to see me and invited me to sit in the pulpit with the rest of the ministers.

On my last Sunday in Cleveland, my pastor asked me to give a thirty-minute sermon to the congregation about my experience in war and what was it like defending the Holy Land in the war. My sermon was more like a talk. My sermon was titled "Knocking Down Giants in Your Life." I used the Bible verses 1 Samuel 17:48, 49, and 50:

> As the Philistine moved closer to attack him, David ran quickly toward the battle line to meet him. Reaching into his bag and taking out a stone, he slung it and struck the Philistine on the forehead. The stone sank into his forehead, and he fell face down on the ground. So, David triumphed over the Philistine with a sling and a stone; without a sword in his hand, he struck down the Philistine and killed him.

I spoke about the Patriot missile launchers being the modern-day slingshot as they launched into the air Patriot missiles, just like David's slingshot slung the stones into the air and killed the giant Goliath. This time the Patriot missile was the giant killer. The weapon that we used, just like David's stone, delivered a death blow to Saddam Hussein's giant master plan. The Patriot missiles shot down the Iraqi Scud missiles headed to Israel for the purpose of killing and terrorizing the children of Israel, just like Goliath terrorized the Israelites (1 Sam. 17:40–

135

49). I then spoke on the many sites that I visited in Israel, like Haifa, the Sea of Galilee (where many of our soldiers were given the opportunity to be baptized), Tel Aviv, and Capernaum (the Town of Jesus where Jesus conducted the Sermon of the Mount and preached the Beatitudes). I also discussed our visit to Jerusalem, where we visited the remnants of the Second Temple and Holocaust Memorial Museum. I ended my visit with my walk down the winding street of Via Dolorosa, which was the processional route of Jesus on the way to the cross. I ended my talk by saying, "You too can defeat the giants in your life." The congregation was amazed by my experience and what I had done as a soldier and an ambassador for Christ. It felt good when many of the church members still remembered me as that young polite serviceman.

On August 18, my family and I departed Cleveland for the 1,752- mile journey (or three and a half days) to El Paso, Texas. It took us two and days and 937 miles to drive through all of Ohio, Kentucky, Tennessee, and Arkansas before we reached the Texas state borders. I made it my mission, while driving to Texas, to look out for famous churches and ministries, especially in the big cities, on our way to El Paso. It was my plan to see all the unique churches that I could see on the way. I was hoping to see Church in God in Christ's Temple of Deliverance Church (pastored by Bishop Patterson) in Memphis, Tennessee. I did find his church location on my map. We got pretty close to his church, but the traffic was too congested and the highway leading toward his church was backed up, so we decided to proceed to Arkansas. Being that it was August, it was extremely hot. The 1988 Chevrolet sedan's air conditioner was starting to work intermittently as soon as we crossed the Arkansas border into Texas.

We still had 815 miles, a two-day drive, to go before we were scheduled to arrive in El Paso. By this time, Tammy and the kids were irritated. We rolled down all four windows, trying to get some relief. That was fine in the morning, but the afternoon heat made it too hot. I prayed to God for some relief. There were several times that I really got worried that the car was going to overheat, and I was terrified that we were going to break down in the middle of nowhere on a desert highway. Boy, I prayed to God for a hedge of protection, and I asked Him to send my guardian angel to protect us along the way. I did all the driving while my family slept most of the time. We soon arrived in Dallas–Fort Worth area. I wanted to see all the different churches on the way to El Paso. Dallas had some well-known pastors like Tony Evans and Dr. Robert Jeffress, just to name a few. I was hoping to see their churches too, but I could not because Tammy was still irritated and just wanted to get to El Paso as soon as possible. A couple of hours later, we were now halfway through Texas, with five hundred more miles to go. The only thing that we saw for most of the remaining miles was the hot sun, the heat wave coming off the highway, armadillos, snakes, cactus plants, and all those huge tumbleweeds that blew across the highway.

We finally completed our 1,752-mile drive and arrived in El Paso, Texas, in the late afternoon. We were relieved when we saw the sign that said, "Welcome to El Paso." A mile later we saw another big colorful sign showing a coyote lying down on his belly next to a big cactus plant in the shade with its tongue on the ground that said, "Welcome to El Paso. Its 105 degrees in the shade." We laughed at the sign and was glad that our trip was coming to an end. We prayed and thanked God that our car held up through the hot desert sun and that we arrived safely to El Paso. We drove to the main gate of Fort Bliss. The sign said, "Welcome to Fort Bliss, The Home of the Air Defense Artillery Soldier and the Home of 3rd Armor Cav Regiment." We signed into the Fort Bliss guest house. We were excited to be back at Fort Bliss but exhausted from the three-day long drive. All I could remembers is carrying all our bags to the room and lying down on the bed. Tammy said that I was so tired that I immediately fell to sleep for four hours. Tammy and the kids went outside to play on the swings and got something to eat while I slept. Being that we were now in El Paso, we had to make the time zone adjustment from Eastern Standard Time to Mountain Time, which has a two-hour time difference.

The following day, I had to process in and receive my assignment. The assignment team initially assigned me to a Patriot missile battalion that just replaced my battalion in Saudi Arabia. This meant that once I processed into my new unit, I would have been sent immediately back to Saudi Arabia. This would have been a horrible assignment. I went out to my car and used it as a phone booth to make a quick call to Jesus so that He could supernaturally intervene and change my assignment. I returned to the building and asked to speak to someone about my assignment.

I explained my situation to the officer that was over the assignment section. He understood and assigned me to the Patriot missile training battalion to be an instructor at the 16 Tango Patriot missile course. This was an advanced individual training course that trained soldiers that just completed their basic training and current soldiers that reenlisted for this new job.

My new job was training them on how to operate and set up the Patriot missile's launchers and radar system. Boy, did I catch a break. You better believe that I thanked Jesus for stepping in. This was definitely a hallelujah moment.

Within three months, I was appointed chief instructor over the entire Patriot missile launcher crewmen course. My new assignment was to train new instructors and supervise forty-two instructors that were sergeants (E-5s), staff sergeants (E-6s), and sergeant first classes (E-7s). My job also required me to write and develop new training lesson plans for the course. Being that I was

138

now the chief instructor, I had the overall responsibility for the safety of every trainee or new soldier that had to go through our training course. I was personally responsible to account for over ten million dollars in Patriot missile s y s t e m equipment and the training center's properties.

My family had to stay at the guest house for the first three weeks while we waited to be assigned Army housing. We were finally given a beautiful ranch-style quarters at the sergeant majors' housing area. The housing area had senior sergeant E-7 and above living there with their families. The housing area was located within walking distance to the Chihuahua Desert that surround the city of El Paso. This location was perfect for walking or running and spending my private time with God on these desert dirt roads. The only thing that I had to watch out for was a few tarantulas, snakes, centipedes, and other desert creatures that would occasionally cross my path while I was running. After a while I started calling them my friends. Every now and then I would come across another soldier that was running out there too. There were times that I would get a little bothered by the sight of a few cayotes that I could hear howling in the distance.

My first week in El Paso, I prayed for God to send me to a church that could use my service as a minister. I believed in my heart that God directed me to a nondenominational church called Temple Church of Deliverance. The pastor's name was Pastor James Lewis. He appeared at first to be a man after God's heart. He accepted the letter of good standing from my previous pastor, Pastor Gadson. Pastor Lewis and I prayed for God's guidance. Afterward, he gave me an interview, reviewed my minister's credentials, and asked me about my experience as a minister. Pastor Lewis said that he has never accepted another minister that he did not know; however, he was willing to accept me as one of his ministers because he understood the difficulties that serviceman and servicewomen had in staying in one location and with one church. Pastor Lewis introduced me to all the other ministers. They were happy to have me join their team.

He invited me to sit in the pulpit with the rest of the ministers during my first Sunday. I had to go through a two-week ministerial training program before I was allowed to teach or preach at this church. After I completed the program, Pastor Lewis allowed me to lead the church services in prayer and conduct adult Sunday school and several Wednesday-night Bible study classes. I was happy, and I was learning a lot from Pastor Lewis and the other ministers. Within six months, I was ordained a minister. Church life for me was going well too. It was about nine months after I joined the Church of Deliverance ministerial team when thing started getting weird. Money, which is said to be the root of all evil, started rearing its ugly head in our church.

Pastor Lewis started putting pressure on the congregation to raise more money for the church-building fund, church mortgage, a new church van, and other pet projects that Pastor Lewis wanted done. One Bible study turned into an attempted demon-casting-out session. Pastor Lewis had several of the church members picked up a homeless lady. They bought her to the Bible study service. We welcomed her and made her feel at home. We were about a half hour into the service when Pastor Lewis asked several of the ushers to bring the homeless lady to the church altar for prayers. Immediately, Pastor Lewis stood in front of the lady and congregation announcing that the lady was demon possessed.

Pastor Lewis asked the lady's name and explained to the lady that he wanted to cast the demon out to set her free. He then orders two ministers to stand behind her to hold her in place. She struggled with them, causing them all to fall to the ground while they held her down on the ground so that Pastor Lewis could speak to the demon and cast it out of her. After fifteen minutes of hearing the lady crying and literately begging to be let go and Pastor Lewis talking to the alleged demon, who refused to say anything, identify itself, or even come out, Pastor Lewis suddenly declared the lady to be demon free.

We all clapped, some did a praised dance, and we all praised the Lord, because, according to Pastor Lewis, this woman was set free from the bondage of this demon. He then asked for a collection to put the lady into a hotel for the night and to get her a decent meal. The church collected 138 dollars with the purpose of getting her something to eat and putting her up into a hotel for the night. My spirit told me that this was not scriptural. I was not comfortable about what had just happened. It appeared to me more like an assault than a healing. I went home that night following the service feeling bad for the lady, but I felt good knowing that tonight she would at least get something good to eat and have a good night's sleep in a hotel because of the money that was collected for her.

Gulf War Illness Jesus Is My Healer

The following Sunday, Pastor Lewis declared during the service that he had power over the devil as he was able to cast out a demon that was in the homeless lady during our Bible study class. Again, the church celebrated what we believed was a victory over the enemy. Later in the week, during our Wednesday minister's meeting, which we have prior to our weekly Bible study class, I overheard a conversation between two of our senior ministers. They were laughing and boasting that they gave the homeless lady ten bucks, then dropped her butt on the street where they found her. She never did stay in the hotel as promised. I felt sorry for the homeless lady and bad for our senior ministers and what our church failed to do in its promise to the lady. My spirit told me Pastor Lewis was aware and had condoned what happened to this lady.

I was disappointed. I must confess that I was caught up in the moment when this was going on and had a small role in this spectacle by witnessing and praying in the spirit as this was going on. I knew in my spirit that this was wrong when this was happening. But could not speak out because I was really hoping deep down in my spirit that if she did have a demon that Pastor Lewis would be able to cast it out. I could no longer be a minister in this church. The Spirit of the Lord told me that it was time to leave this church and to move on to somewhere else. I spoke with Pastor Lewis the following day to express my concerns and to asked him to release me as one of his ministers because I felt that God was sending me onto another assignment. We prayed, and we thanked each other for the time that we served together. Pastor Lewis hugged me and said, "I love you, brother." He said that if I changed my mind that I would be welcome to come back. Pastor Lewis released me from being a minister at this church. I loved Pastor Lewis and still do even to this day.

I prayed again to the Lord for a new church home that could use my services as a minister for God's kingdom. This time I felt in my spirit that God directed me to the Visitor's Chapel African Methodist Episcopal (AME) Church. I drove by the church that Saturday afternoon before the service to read the church's bulletin information board. I felt that this is where God wanted me to be. The pastor's name was Pastor Williams. The information board said that there is a Sunday school that starts at 10:00 a.m. with a morning worship service that starts at 11:00 a.m. I headed back home, asking God on the way, "Is this where you want me to be?" God didn't answer me, so I assumed that He said yes. Why else would He sent me to visit the church that Saturday? I got up early the next day and went on my usual spiritual run in the cool desert sun of El Paso in the morning in preparation for their Sunday school.

I did not want to be late, so I arrived at 9:45 a.m. The first thing that I notice as I arrived was that the parking lot in front of the church was empty of cars. There were two cars parked on the side. I went ahead and walked into the sanctuary hoping to see if there was someone that I might know from Fort Bliss. No one was there. Then 10:00 a.m. arrived. It was time for the Sunday school to start. Still there was no one there. It was 10:30 a.m. when the pastor came out of the attached parsonage where he and his family lived. He came to the sanctuary to pray and prepare for the Sunday church service. He was surprised and embarrassed to see me sitting there.

We spoke briefly about the church, my experience as a minister, and my job as a soldier at Fort Bliss. I showed him my wallet-size ordination credential. He asked me if I were interested in speaking with him more after the service because he had been praying that God would send him some help. He said that he was the only minister at this church. I agreed to meet with him after the service.

Soon, at 10:45 a.m., members of the congregation started to arrive. Majority of the members were senior citizens, over fifty, with a few young adults in their thirties. The only two teenagers in the service were Pastor Williams's teenage daughter and young son. No children attended this service. There were fifty members that were in attendance. Pastor Williams announced during the church announcements that there will be an adult Sunday school service starting back next Sunday.

I thought that it was odd that he invited the members to be there, as if the last Sunday school was some time ago. The members looked surprised too. Some were glad to hear his announcement. I was announced as a guess minister during the church announcements. I spoke to the congregation about myself and praised God for allowing me to be in their service. The service was good but stiff. The congregation seemed to enjoy the service that clearly lacked the presence of the Holy Spirit. The service lasted a little over an hour.

I met with Pastor Williams and his family after the service. He asked me if I was interested in coming back. He invited me to teach the next Sunday school service as a guess minister. I agreed. He gave me a copy of the Sunday school journal so that I could prepare.

The following Sunday, fifteen church members showed up for Sunday school. I think mostly to see who was teaching the class. The class went well. The following week more people started showing up. Everyone was happy with my enthusiasm. They were glad to restart their Sunday school program. By my third week, a new minister named Mike Reed showed up to assist Pastor Williams. He too was in the Army at Fort Bliss. He was here to attend the sergeant major's academy. Pastor Williams invited both of us to sit in the pulpit to help him conduct the services. Pastor Williams said to the congregation that he thanked God for finally sending him the help for which he was praying for.

Two week later, Minister Reed and I both approached Pastor Williams about the lack of youth and kids in the services. He agreed, so we developed a plan to encourage the members to start bringing their young family members back to church. Minister Mike Reed took over the adult Sunday school, and I started teaching the youth Sunday school. The following Sunday, we had twenty kids in Sunday school. This included my three kids as well. The kids enjoyed the Sunday school but were too jumpy, obviously bored, and could not sit still enough in the church service for the older congregates. Another two weeks later, Pastor Williams appointed me as the youth pastor. We began a youth church service in the lower level of the church. Everyone was happy. The church attendance started to grow both in the adult and youth services. Minister Reed and I would go with Pastor Williams to make hospital visits to pray for our hospitalized church members or someone that was on our prayer list. We would also visit our church members that were on our sick and shut-in list to pray for them and to provide Holy Communion for them too. Pastor Williams was proud of our accomplishments.

Soon it was time for Pastor Williams to rotate to another church within the state of Texas. Pastors in the AME churches are considered itinerant pastors, meaning that they must rotate to another church every three to four years. We received a new pastor, Rev. Thomas Ates, who came to us from Austin, Texas. Pastor Ates was a gifted preacher with a lot of enthusiasm. Being in El Paso was a step down for him when it came down to the size of the congregation and living in the church parsonage as compared to the generous size of the church and a single-family parsonage that he lived in while he was pastoring at the Austin AME Church. He often bragged about the horses he had in Austin. I loved Pastor Ates and the changes he was making to the church. I was proud when I was invited to teach during the El Paso All City

Ministerial Alliance Conference that year. The subject that I taught was on biblical marriage and the family. I used Genesis 1:28 as my teaching text.

My job in the Army was going good as well. Suddenly, I started getting sick in 1995. My headaches and muscle aches that I had while I was in Germany started getting much worse. I started having breathing issues too. Here I was, a senior sergeant, thirty-six years old, and known as one of my unit's main cadence callers that would lead the formation singing songs on our fitness runs. I was also quick and could run a two-mile run in less than twelve minutes. I was now starting to have trouble keeping up during unit's fitness runs due to my breathing issues. Things started getting worse when I noticed that I was becoming fatigue and had lack the strength to do simple task. I was having difficulties climbing stairs too. I thought about going on sick call the next day but decided that I would wait a week because I was already scheduled to take a complete physical examination for the Gulf War registry. This is an examination that the Army wanted all soldiers that participated in the Gulf War to do. This was done to track our health because soldiers were starting to die from unknown causes while others were starting to develop unknown sickness believed to be caused by being in the Gulf War. By now this sickness was being called Persian Gulf War syndrome. I was having some of the same symptoms too, but I did not really think that this applied to me because I did not go to the Gulf region of Saudi Arabia, Kuwait, or Iraq during the war.

I took my Gulf War physical examination on August 3, 1995, at the base's main dispensary. Everything seems normal at first until the doctor read my chest X-ray. He seemed alarmed when he read it. He immediately asked me the strangest questions like how long you have been smoking and what type of cigarettes do you smoke. I felt offended by his questions. I had to pause for a second to catch my breath. I was stunned by his questions. I responded, "Sir,

I have never smoked a cigarette in a day of my life, and I have always been careful of secondhand smoke." He was surprised by my answer. He then asked me where I was at during the war. I told him Israel and then a year later in Saudi Arabia. He seemed surprised by this answer too. He then instructed me to have a seat in the hallway while he made a call to the pulmonary clinic at the Fort Bliss Army hospital. He came back a few minutes later. He handed me a sealed envelope that contained my chest X-ray. He ordered me to go directly to the pulmonary clinic at the hospital. By now, I was in a panic mode. I got into my car and drove to the hospital. Sweat was coming from my forehead. To be honest, I was scared as hell because I did not know what was so concerning to the doctor.

I arrived at the hospital. I reported directly to the pulmonary clinic per instructions from the doctor at the dispensary. Dr. Wallingford, a lieutenant colonel, was the chief pulmonary doctor in this clinic. He came out to greet me. He said that he has been waiting for me to arrive. I handed him the envelope that contained my chest X-ray and medical records. He took them and told me to have a seat. He said he will need to see my X-ray and medicals. He said that he will be

right back. It was alarming to me several minutes later when I could hear him paging the rest of the doctors that were working at the time in the pulmonary clinic to his office so that they could all see my chest X-ray. Several minutes later, after looking, reviewing, and discussing my chest X-ray, I could see the doctors with their heads down, and none of them looked at me as if they were afraid to do so, like I had some type of communicable disease. Dr. Wallingford came out and asked me to come into his office. He had my chest X- ray on display in his office. I was startled when he said, "We have been waiting for someone to show up that went to the Gulf War with problems with their lungs." He then tried to comfort me by saying that I look like a nice guy and that he was sorry that this happen

147

to me. He then showed me my X-rays and explained to me that I have gaping holes in my lungs, which is similar to a patient that has tuberculosis or some other mycobacterium illness.

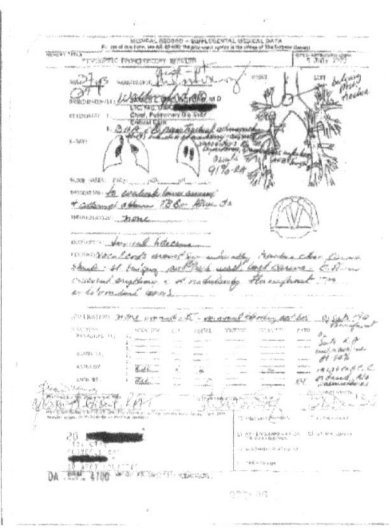

Medical record

Dr. Wallingford then said that both are potentially serious infectious diseases that affects the lungs. Dr. Wallingford then asked me about my symptoms and when was I in Kuwait during the oil fires. He was shocked when I explained to him, just like I told the other doctor at the dispensary, that I served in Israel during Operations Desert Storm and then I was deployed a year later in Saudi Arabia. Dr. Wallingford then looked surprised. He then asked me if I remembered being bitten by a sandfly while I was in Saudi. I responded I don't think so. He then said that it was getting late and that the clinic is closing soon for the day. He said that my symptoms at this time are mild and that I was not going to die anytime soon. But he did have some serious concerns about the condition of my lungs. He said that I could go home for the night, but he needed me to come back as soon as the clinic opened at 7:30 a.m. because he needed to run test and do a biopsy to determine what is going on in my lungs. I departed the clinic fearful of tomorrow. I wept and I prayed to God for a healing. Crazy thoughts were racing through my mind like death, what will happen to my wife and kids, and who will take my place as Tammy's new husband and the stepfather of my kids.

I arrived home, but I was too afraid to tell Tammy that night because I did not want to scare her or have her worrying without knowing exactly what was going on with my health. The next day I got up. I went for a prayer walk in the desert, and I asked Doctor Jesus to heal me and that I needed a good report after all the tests were done. I arrived at the hospital as instructed by Dr. Wallingford. All the tests were done. The biopsy was painful. It took two weeks for me to get my report back. Dr. Wallingford's diagnosis for me was pulmonary sarcoidosis, which is a chronic lung disease. Dr. Wallingford put me on a treatment program that consisted of medicines and a steroid called prednisone. It was now time to tell Tammy about my sickness and the medical program that I was put on. She was hurt that I did not tell her sooner but was glad that I have a Father-son relationship with God. We prayed, touched, agreed, and declared with me that I would be healed soon. Tammy agreed that she would help in my healing process too. I continued with the treatment that Dr. Wallingford put me on.

Despite the fact that I was having several episodes of shortness of breath and I was also having periods of the lack of strength, Pastor Ates still wanted me to preach the Sunday morning service.

We prayed that the Holy Spirit would strengthen me to finish my sermon. I recited to myself Philippians 4:13 that says, "I can do all things through Christ who strengthens me." Having the words of the apostle Paul gave me the strength to finish my sermon. I prepared and studied all week for it. My sermon title was "Do You Have a Zeal for God or Are You a Great Pretender?" My Bible verse came from Romans 10:1–2:

> Brethren, my heart's desire and prayed to God for Israel is that they may be saved. For I bear them witness that they have a zeal for God, but not according to knowledge.

I got up that morning and went on my Sunday morning desert prayer walk to pray for strength and to practice out loud my sermon to the desert creatures that by now I was calling my friends. Prior to practicing my sermon, I wanted to get pumped up by listening to the Christian radio station. Betty Robinson, the Sunday morning hostess who attend the same AME church that I attended and also our organist, was playing some good praise and worship gospel music this morning that was speaking to my spirit. Between songs, Betty made an announcement over the airwaves that she was praying for Reverend Glover, who scheduled to preach this morning at Visitor's Chapel AME Church. I was surprised and happy that Betty had announced my name on the radio.

The next song that Betty played was a song by Milton Brunson and the Thompson Community choir. The name of the song is called "I'm Free." Milton Brunson elevated his already strong-sounding voice to a thunderous shout when he sang this line in the song: *"Praise the Lord, hallelujah I'm free. I am saved and sanctified and filled with the fire. I'm free. Born-again, born again, Jeremiah said I can feel the fire moving, moving in my bones."*

I started singing and shouting the lyrics with him. I immediately felt the presence of the Holy Spirit and a warming sensation racing through my lungs. I got a little scared because I could tell that something was happening in my body. I then felt a gentle, warm breeze and something that was gently pushing me from behind. I got a little scared by the pushes, so I put my hands up in a defensive karate position, and I quickly turned around to see if there was someone behind me. There was no one behind me. I continued with my walk. I took a few more steps, then I felt the gentle, warm breeze and those pushes again. This time I did not look behind me but started running, just like anyone else would have done not knowing what was pushing them from behind.

I started to notice that I was now running and I was no longer having difficulty breathing, so I ran a little faster and a little farther. It felt amazing just to be running again. I started shouting in the top of my lungs in English, and then I finished shouting in tongues, declaring, "I am healed. I am healed. Thank God Almighty. I am healed." I ran the two remaining miles back home from my desert walk, which now turned into my desert run. I was rejoicing and praising God the rest of the way. As I got closer to the house, I noticed that Tammy was outside playing with the kids in the front yard. I ran past the house, waving at Tammy, trying to get her attention so that she could see that I was now running. I had to run in a circle twice in front of our house before Tammy realized that I was running. When she did notice, she started smiling and shouting, "Hallelujah! Praise the Lord!" knowing that I was healed.

I often wondered to myself afterward, even to this day, if that gentle, warm breeze that I felt behind me that day was this the breath of the Holy Spirit and if that gentle push from behind were the hands of the Holy Spirit or a heavenly angel with the purpose of getting my attention to acknowledge that I was being healed. All I knew was that from that moment when my lungs were healed, I declared and I claimed my healing in the healing name of Jesus. From that day and for several days after I received healing, I was on a spiritual high. I kept on saying, "Thank God Almighty, I am free. Thank God Almighty, I am healed. Amen."

I went to church that morning spiritually ready to declare that the devil's plan to kill me was defeated in this morning in the desert sun. I was fired up and ready to preach my sermon. I was glad that Minister Reed was scheduled to conduct the youth service this morning instead of me. This allowed me to preach to the adult congregation. The church announcements and the choir songs were done. It was now my time to preach my sermon. Pastor Ates turned the pulpit over to me. Prior to conducting my sermon, I announced to the congregation that I had my talk with Doctor Jesus this morning and that he healed me of my lung illness this morning. I declared to them that the devil's plan to kill me was not going to happen. This was the first time that I saw the church members stand up, openly shout, and praised the Lord. I preached my sermon for forty minutes. Several members of the congregation started shouting "Hallelujah" and "Praise the Lord" several times while I preached. This was a surprise to me and to Pastor Ates because the congregation was always silent and lacked spiritual emotion in the past. We were happy at the end of my sermon when two visitors came to the altar to accept the Lord as their savior and then they both joined our church. Amen.

The next day, on Monday morning, I was back in formation running and calling cadences during our battalion's physical training (PT) runs. My soldiers were surprised that I had the breath and strength needed to lead our formation during this run. I had a follow-up appointment with my pulmonary doctor, Dr. Wallingford. He gave me a good report, and he took credit and was proud of the treatment he had put me on. I did not want to bust his bubble, so I never told him about my desert encounter with Doctor Jesus. Dr. Wallingford does deserve some credit for being the human hands that was used by Jesus in my healing process. Amen.

A Time for a Decision

I was so focused on the healing of my lungs that I ignored the occasional pains of the headaches and body aches that were starting to get worse. I started taking pain pills with the expectation that these aches and pains would eventually go away. Jesus healed me of my pulmonary sarcoidosis several months ago, which was a big deal and a miracle to me. I never did ask Jesus to heal me of the aches and pains. I was hoping that the pain pills would do the trick by taking care of the pains. I was so glad that my breathing and running was improving so much that I did not think it was necessary to go back to Doctor Jesus and ask for a healing of my aches and pains.

I figured that I could save the need for another spiritual healing for the future if one were needed or I could use the need for a spiritual healing for the next time that I prayed for someone that was next in line for a miracle. Even though my lungs were healing, I still had to go to the pulmonary clinic every two weeks for my scheduled follow-up appointments so that Dr. Wallingford could monitor my progress. During one of these visits at the pulmonary clinic, I ran into one of my former soldiers who was stationed with me in Germany, Sergeant Davidson. He was at the pulmonary clinic waiting for his appointment to begin. Sergeant Davidson did not go to Israel or to the war with us. He had priority orders that sent him back to the United States to become an Army recruiter. Sergeant Davidson was still in Germany awaiting his departure date when we were deployed. I was told that Sergeant Davidson left for the United States and his recruiting assignment a month after our battalion was deployed to the war.

I was surprised to see Sergeant Davidson at Fort Bliss because he still had more time left on his four-year recruiting duty assignment. We were both glad to see each other. I asked him about his recruiting time. He replied that he hated it and that he only lasted through the one-year recruiting probationary period. He added that he tried his best, but recruiting was too difficult and too demanding on him and his family. He was glad when he got relieved of his recruiting duty. He often regretted that he did not go to war with us. I was so curious why he was in this specific clinic, so I asked him. Sergeant Davison said he was at the clinic because he was having problems with his breathing. His eyes started watering. He said that he was recently diagnosed with a lung disease called pulmonary sarcoidosis and that he was scared and did not know what to expect. I was blown away when he informed me that he too was being treated for pulmonary sarcoidosis. This is the same illness that I was being treated for too. He then said that he was being treated by Dr. Wallingford. It was interesting to know that Sergeant Davidson was not deployed with us to the war; however, he did receive all the different experimental vaccines and medications that we all had to take just in case our Patriot battalion received the word that we had to deploy.

I then informed Sergeant Davidson that I was also diagnosed with pulmonary sarcoidosis and that Dr. Wallingford was my doctor too. He was surprised to hear me say this. I could tell that he felt better knowing that he was not going through this illness alone. We started comparing our lung symptoms. We noticed right away that they were the same. Sergeant Davidson then asked me if I had rashes on my arms and legs. I said no. Sergeant Davidson then asked me, "Do you have headaches and body aches?" I replied yes. By now we were more than convinced that our common illnesses had to come from those experimental vaccines and medications that we had to take in preparation for our expected deployment.

Please understand that I never wanted to give the enemy a victory by claiming pulmonary sarcoidosis as my illness. I always said I was being treated for pulmonary sarcoidosis. I was glad that my lungs were healing. I was still having headaches and muscle aches that started three years ago shortly after my return from the desert of Saudi Arabia back in August 1992. Now my short-term memory was becoming a new, and worse, medical issue for me. I was so focused on my lungs that I put the need to seek treatment for the other ailments on the back burner.

The following week I had a follow-up appointment with Dr. Wallingford. By this time, he had already spoken with Sergeant Davidson on the same day that we saw each other in his clinic, and Dr. Wallingford was fully aware of the conversation that we had and our thoughts about what we believed was the common cause of our illness. Dr. Wallingford stated that they are doing research to understand why we both had the same symptoms. I asked Dr. Wallingford if this was a fluke or just a coincidence, considering that I was deployed to the war but Sergeant Davidson was not.

I was curious to find out why both of us had some of the same symptoms. So, I went on to the web to conduct my own research to see if there was a connection between Gulf War veterans and pulmonary sarcoidosis or any other respiratory disease. There was an internet thread that I found that was forming with inputs from numerous Gulf War veterans that confirmed that they, too, had these respiratory problems. Many of them were contributing their illness to the oil-well fires and the spilled pools of oil that the Iraqi soldiers purposely set on fire while they were retreating from Kuwait prior to the end of the Gulf War. Others blamed the materials that were being burned in the open air that they could smell and were breathing in from those trash burning pits in the Gulf region, while other soldiers like me was blaming our lung problems on the many experimental vaccines and medications that we had to take.

I often wondered what happened to Sergeant Davidson. I never did see him again at Fort Bliss nor did I

155

ever hear from him. I prayed for his healing. I asked God if He could spiritually healed Sergeant Davidson just like he did for me. I felt that Sergeant Davidson was the one that I believed was next in line for a miracle. So, I gave it to God, trusting by faith and believing that my prayers for Sergeant Davidson would not be hindered or blocked by the prince of the airwaves and that Sergeant Davidson will receive his healing in the healing name of Jesus. Amen.

Later that year, the master sergeant E-8 promotion list came out to announce all the sergeant first class E-7s that were selected to be

promoted to master sergeant E-8. I was working as the chief instructor over the Patriot missile crewmen course, which is an E-8 position that I have been working in during the past year. My other assignment as the chief instructor was to brief visiting government dignitaries from Washington, DC, and other VIPs on the Patriot missile system and how effective the system was during the Gulf War. I received excellent comments from the visiting dignitaries about the scope of my briefing and how well the Patriot missile training course was conducted under my leadership.

It was a given but not a guarantee that I would get the promotion to master sergeant E-8. I was disappointed, so was the entire Army chain of command and all my subordinates, when the promotion list was released and my name was not listed among those that were going to get promoted. What made matters worse for me is that five of the sergeant first classes that were currently working under my leadership at Fort Bliss and another sergeant first class that worked for me in Germany were on the promotion list and were to be promoted to master sergeant. Yes, I was devastated when I heard that they made the list, but I was also glad that they made the promotion list to master sergeant.

I was also proud that I played a critical role in helping them all get promoted by giving them all much-deserved high marks on their performance reviews, or Noncommission Officers Evaluation Report (NCOERs). Five of the six were former drill sergeants. I believe this was a key factor on why they got the promotion and I did not. We later found out that Command Sergeant Major Ficklen, who presided over this year's promotion board for E-8, was also an air defense artillery former drill sergeant, battery first sergeant, and a battalion command sergeant major for a Patriot battalion. He also worked with and personally knew five of my six sergeants that were on this year's promotion list. To me this was not fair, but I understood that this was Army politics.

Within a couple of days of the announcement, I was reassigned to a new job within our unit. Since I did not make the promotion list but they did, I could no longer be assigned as their boss or as the chief instructor because I now had five soldiers that worked for me that were now senior to me as promotable E-7(P). This meant that they were going to advance to pay grade E-8, and I was not. Within a couple of days, I was reassigned to another E-7 position within my unit with way less responsibilities. My new job this time was as the noncommissioned officer in charge (NCOIC) of the tools and equipment section. I was not mad with God, nor did I question Him on why I did not make the promotion list to E-8 and why I was passed over for the promotion. The word *passed over* is not the same meaning in the Bible with the death angel or destroyer that passed over the Jewish households in Exodus 12:23. In the Army, *pass over* simply means that you were not selected that year for the promotion.

All was not lost, and it was not a career-ending decision by the Army or a rejection of me because I was not selected this year for a promotion. I had nineteen years in the Army. The average time to get promoted to master sergeant E-8 in my career field was twenty to twenty-one years of service. My spirit reminded me that God is still

157

God and that He is still on the throne and that He being God is still the Commander of my salvation and the Author and Finisher of my life's story. It is just a matter of time that I could get promoted to E-8. My career was still blossoming. I was on track to get promoted to Master Sergeant E-8 on next year's promotion list.

Two weeks later I received orders assigning me to a Patriot battalion in Korea. I had a reporting date to be there in six months. Hell, I just got back from Germany thirteen months ago with two combat tours away from my family during the past two years and now the Army wants me to leave my family again. Going to Korea was a thirteen-month assignment, meaning that as a Patriot soldier, or just like any combat soldier assigned to Korea, you would have been sent close to the Korean demilitarized zone (DMZ). That meant that I could not bring my family with me to Korea. I had a choice to accept this assignment or to retire. I was already disappointed that I did not make the master sergeant list to E-8. I was confused, and I thought that the same Army that did not promote me to E-8 now wants me to go to Korea without my wife and family.

Soon I informed Tammy of the Army's decision to send me to Korea. I was not happy. Neither was Tammy. Tammy and I prayed and consulted with God; and we weighed the pros and cons about me going to Korea, staying in the Army, or to retire. Tammy and I have always functioned as a team, just like every married couple in the Army should. We made the decision together that it was time for us to retire. I can remember hearing my mother's voice that said God works in mysterious ways. I took this as a hint that God had bigger and better plans for me outside the Army. If I did get promoted to E-8, I would have to stay for at least two more years. The promotion to E-8 would have been welcomed, but it would have had delayed God's perfect will and plan for my life.

I have been in the Army since July 11, 1976, I left for basic training twenty-two days after I graduated from high school. The thought of retiring was scary for me. I spent the last nineteen years of my life in the Army, and I loved being in the Army. The Army is all that I knew. The following day I filled out all the necessary paperwork to begin the retirement process. I requested a retirement date of September 1, 1996. The Army was good in preparing soldiers for retirement. I had to go through a physical examination, resume writing classes, family planning seminars, and schedule the day for my furniture to be picked up and sent to the city and state where I was planning on living after my retirement. We had to make a choice to stay in El Paso, move to New Jersey (where I was from), or to move to Cleveland (where Tammy was from). We decided that El Paso was too hot, too far away from our families, and the average job paid you $10 an hour. New Jersey was too expensive and too stormy in the spring and summer months. We already lived in Cleveland. Tammy's family was too big, and we did not want to be caught up in their family politics. We still had time to decide where.

Decision Made—Time to Retire from the Army

One Sunday after church service, I was watching TV when a church service came on featuring a loudmouthed screaming White preacher from the cornfields of Columbus, Ohio, declaring what I took as a clarion call to go to Columbus, Ohio, to attend World Harvest's Bible College's School of the Spirit. I was amazed by his fire and his teaching of the Holy Spirit. He reminded me of my preaching idols R. W. Schambach and Reverend Ike. For the next several weeks, I watched Pastor Rod Parsley spit out fiery sermons and deliver the gospel truth. He had that fire and spark that I wanted to have for my ministry. I got with Tammy, and she started watching his services with me. She enjoyed his preaching style too. My desire to go to World Harvest Bible College helped us to make the decision to temporarily move to Columbus, Ohio. Our goal was to move somewhere in two years after I completed my Bible college training.

Tammy and I prayed and fasted for twenty-four hours for guidance from the Holy Spirit about my decision to attend World Harvest Bible College after my retirement from the Army. We both received our confirmation from the Holy Spirit that this was His plan for us. Next, I had to notify Fort Bliss's household goods section that our furniture will need to be shipped to Columbus. The hardest notification I had to make was informing the youth that I was pastoring at Visitor's Chapel AME Church and my spiritual father Pastor Ates that I was retiring in a couple of months and that I have plans to move away from El Paso and that my family was moving to Columbus, Ohio, where I was planning on attending World Harvest Bible College instead of the AME Church's Wilberforce University also in Ohio. I met with Pastor

160

Ates that Wednesday evening thirty minutes prior to our midweek Bible study class. I was also the Bible study teacher scheduled for this day.

Pastor Ates congratulated me for my service to the country and for my decision to retire. He was not happy with my decision to move away from El Paso or the thought of me attending a Bible College outside the AME church denominational structure. Pastor Ates suggested that I should go back and pray again and reconsider my decision to attend Wilberforce University. By now my decision to attend World Harvest Bible College was already made with the help of the Holy Spirit and Tammy. That Sunday after the youth service was over, I informed them too that I was leaving. Several of the youth started crying while some of the other youths became sad because they did not want me or my children to leave. I made a promise to them that God had a plan for them and that soon another minister would take my place.

I loved ministering at the Visitor's Chapel, AME Church. I was also proud of my accomplishments serving God's people there, especially the young kids and the teenagers at this church. My time there and my association with the AME church was only for a season. I felt that God used me to add fire back into this congregation, which, I am proud to say, that I did. There were also some things and practices that I thought that was not beneficial to me and my family in the long term if I decided to stay in the AME church as a minister. I felt that the AME church was quenching the power of the Holy Spirit. I must admit that there were many positive things that I loved about serving as a minister and youth pastor at Visitor's Chapel. My future goal was to one day pastor my own ministry or church, preferably a nondenominational Spirit-filled ministry or church.

As ministers or representatives of Christ, I am sure that we all had said this same statement or prayer at one time or another: "God sent me. I will go." By making this statement or prayer, you have agreed with Jesus's

161

commandment in Matthew 28:16–20, the Great Commission, wherein Jesus commands that we all *"Go."* It is my opinion that Jesus said, "Go somewhere to spread the gospel." Jesus, also in my opinion, gave us another directive in Matthew 9:36 when He said to his disciples, "The harvest truly is plenteous, but the laborers are few." I took it that the Lord of the Harvest was saying that we are all farmers in the Great Harvest and that we must go somewhere to labor in gathering up his harvest, which are those that he has called. Amen.

We also must be mindful of the Holy Spirit and understand the path that he had predestined for us to travel. The fact is that every believer of Christ is a minister and an ambassador for Christ regardless of whether you are licensed, ordained, or simply a follower of Christ. Do you remember what the apostle Paul wrote in 2 Corinthians 5:18 (NIV)? He said, "All this is from God, who reconciled us to himself through Christ and gave us the ministry of reconciliation." Let me make this clear. Every believer has a part in the ministry of reconciliation. One plants; one waters, and God brings the increase according to 1 Corinthians 3:7. We are all God's representatives. Amen.

My relationship and my ability to speak to God and to hear from Him began at the age of five on the same day when President Kennedy was assassinated and my best friend, Brian's father was killed in an automobile accident on November 22, 1963. The first church that I attended at the age of ten was the Messiah Lutheran Church in my hometown of Plainfield, New Jersey. I gave my life to Christ at this church. Several months later, I was baptized on the same day with my other brothers and sisters. Since then, I have been a member and a minister in a Baptist church, a nondenominational church, a Church of God in Christ Church, and now with an African Methodist Episcopal Church. I have been blessed by God by allowing these pastors of these churches to accept my ministerial credentials to serve in their churches as a traveling minister and as a soldier. It was the power of God that allowed me to learn and grow spiritually from each of these different denominations as a minister and member. It is interesting that now that I am leaving the Army, God is sending me to a Pentecostal church and Bible college in Columbus, Ohio. My spirit told me that if God is not a respecter of persons, He is surely not a respecter of man-inspired denominations.

The Bible truth is that we who confess to be followers of Christ are all Christians. Many believers don't realize that they are either an Orthodox, Catholic, or a Protestant Christian, which are considered the three main branches of Christianity. Here is another fact as to why many Christians don't really know or understand why they attend a specific denomination.

There are over two hundred different Christian denominations or Christian subgroups in the United States and well over forty-five thousand different Christian denominations worldwide. The spirit in me never felt bound by a denominational church. Jesus has never instructed any of us to "Go" to a Baptist church or "Go" to a Lutheran church or "Go to any specific denominational church. In reality, I was always destined to belong to a nondenominational church. A nondenominational church or ministry is a Christian church or ministry that holds no connection to a denominational church structure such as the Baptist, Catholic, Lutheran, Methodist, or Presbyterian churches or follow beliefs, methodology, theology, or traditional practices. Jesus also never said you need to be a conservative or a liberal Christian. I never wanted to be caught up with religious dogma. All I know is that I love Jesus and I just want to preach and teach Jesus and Him crucified according to what the apostle Paul said in 1 Corinthians 2:2 (NIV): "For I resolved to know nothing while I was with you except Jesus Christ and Him crucified."

On July 13, 1996, Tammy and I took part in Fort Bliss's retirement ceremony and parade. We walked side by side on the parade field with all the retiring soldiers and their spouses. It was nice when we walked in front of the reviewing stand filled with Fort Bliss's leadership team, visiting dignitaries, and the crowd of family members and friends that wanted to watch the ceremony from the stands. Tammy and I looked at each other and smiled when it was our turn to walk in front of the crowd. It was heartwarming when the announcer said our names as retiring Sergeant First Class Lloyd C. Glover and his spouse, Mrs. Tammy C. Glover.

The crowd cheered and clapped when the post's commanding general of Fort Bliss presented me with the Meritorious Service Medal (MSM), which is a military award presented to members of the United States Armed Forces who distinguished themselves by outstanding meritorious achievement or service to the United States.

The commanding general then presented Tammy with a certificate of appreciation signed by President Bill Clinton for her support as a soldier's spouse. We were both proud of our achievements and the awards that we were presented with by the post commanding general. We had a small retirement party later that day with my soldiers and our closest friends.

Even though Tammy and I took part in the retirement ceremony that day, I will not officially retire from the Army until September 1, 1996. As of this day, I was no longer required to attend formations or required to wear the Army uniforms. The good thing about going through the retirement ceremony on July 23 was that I will still get paid my full military paycheck until September 1 when I would be officially retired from the Army. I also had vacation days and travel time that I will need to use up prior to September 1. Now that the retirement celebrations were over, it was now time for me to say goodbye to Pastor Ates, who also was my friend and my spiritual father, and the Visitor

164

Chapel's congregation and the youth church that I pastored and love so much. This was the hardest goodbye that I ever had to do. Pastor Ates allowed me to preach on my last Sunday. Pastor Ates thanked me for my service to the church. The youth church came into the sanctuary at the end of my sermon. The youth church presented me with a going-away plaque that read,

> Presented to Youth
> Pastor Lloyd C.
> Glover. We are
> going to miss you.
> Much Love from the Youth at Visitor's Chapel AME
> Church.

I was puzzled when Pastor Ates announced to the congregation that I was going to Wilberforce University when he knew clearly that I was going to World Harvest Bible College. I guess he was hoping that I did change my mind. After the service was over, we celebrated my service to the church with a going-away party. Everyone at the party hugged me, wished me to be successful, and said their final goodbyes.

We had two days left in El Paso before we had to leave. We decided that we were going to visit my family first in New Jersey for two weeks and then to Cleveland for a week or two. After these family visits, we will head to Columbus to begin our new life after the Army. The day before we left, I had to visit my desert friends and creatures in the Chihuahua Desert to say goodbye. I did not run for the last time but decided to walk instead because I wanted to cherish my final talk with Jesus in my secret place in El Paso, which was my desert open-air closet.

I started by listening to a few praise and worship songs, and I began to speak in my heavenly language, worshiping and thanking Jesus for the times that I spend at Fort Bliss and El Paso. I asked God for the protection of the families at Visitor's Chapel AME Church and for another spirit-filled minister that has a love for God and for the youth to replace me as soon as possible to keep the young people encouraged. I asked for protection of my family and for traveling mercies as we began our journey back home.

The last thing that I did ask of Jesus was for my acceptance to World Harvest Bible College and for a job in Columbus, Ohio, making at least ten dollars an hour that would supplement my retirement check so that I could provide for my family while I attend Bible college. I believed in my spirit that God said yes to my request.

Preparing for Life outside of the Army

The following morning on July 15, 1996, we packed up our van with our luggage and our four kids to begin our 2,159-mile trip from El Paso back to my hometown of Plainfield, New Jersey. Based on my calculations, it should take us four days to get to Plainfield from here. We prayed for traveling mercies and a hedge of protection prior to us starting our journey at 4:00 a.m. I wanted to start my drive when it was the coolest part of the morning and also get us a five-hour head start on the hot and rising Texas sun. The Texas sun would start getting hot as early as 9:00 a.m. Tammy and I learned our lessons from previous trips of starting our trips midmorning, around 9:00 a.m., and then driving through the hot desert sun. That was not smart. Our plans for this day were to drive 665 miles all the way to the Dallas–Fort Worth area, where we planned to stop midafternoon and to rest for the evening so that we could get an early start for the second day of our journey. Being that all our kids were young, I had to plan breaks during our trip for our kids as well.

I also brought Bible study cassette lessons with me so that I could listen to and study the Word of God while I drove each day. I wanted to take advantage of the times, especially when my family was asleep. I brought with me several different Bible study lessons to choose from like the "Fivefold Ministry Gifts," "Bible History," and the "Gifts of the Holy Spirit." I chose to study the nine gifts of the Spirit first to keep me alert during our trip and to help prepare me for Bible college. My plan to start with the nine gifts of the Spirit, which was a good place to start. The gifts of the Spirit are simply God empowering faithful Christians to do and equip us for what He has called us to do. You could find the nine gifts of the Holy Spirit in 1 Corinthians 12:4–11 (NIV):

There are various kinds of gifts, but the same Spirit distributes them. There are different kinds of service, but the same Lord. There are different kinds of working, but in all of them and in everyone it is the same God at work. now to each one the manifestation of the Spirit is given for the common good. To one there is given through the Spirit a message of wisdom, to another a message of knowledge by means of the same Spirit, to another faith by the same Spirit, to another gifts of healing by that one Spirit, to another miraculous powers, to another prophecy, to another distinguishing between spirits, to another speaking in different kinds of tongues, and to still another the interpretation of tongues, All these are the work of one and the same Spirit, and he distributes them to each one, just as he determines.

I learned from these lessons that the gifts of the Spirit are broken down into three categories, which are the revelation gifts, the power gifts, and the speaking gifts. Each category has three gifts and a specific spiritual purpose. My goal was to study one of the categories each day, which included their three gifts of the Spirit and the purpose of their spiritual meanings. Every Christian has been empowered with a spiritual gift or gifts. Read what is written in 1 Peter 4:10 about us being given spiritual gifts: "God has given each of you a gift from his great variety of spiritual gifts. Use them well to serve one another."

I was hoping by the time that I finished studying the gifts of the Spirit, I would gain a better understanding of the gifts and that the Holy Spirit would give me a revelation of which gift that He has given me to operate in. Amen.

The first day while driving through Texas, I focused on the three revelation gifts, which are the gifts of wisdom, knowledge, and discerning of spirits. I learned that the gift

168

of _the word of wisdom_ is a spiritual gift that is designed to enable the believer who receive this gift to know things that they would not know otherwise without the help of the Holy Spirit. This gift manifests itself as a supernatural impartation of a future events or to have knowledge of something in advance. The second gift that I focused on was _the word of knowledge_. The word of knowledge is a spiritual gift given to believers by the Holy Spirit. It is a supernatural knowledge that manifests as a vision, dream, thought, voice, or feeling. The word of knowledge is a revelatory gift and often works together with other gifts of the Spirit. The third gift that I focused on was _the discerning of spirits_. This gift equips the believer to see and discern evil spirits that are operating in and around someone's life and to see what spirits that are trying to attack the believer simply because they are a child of God and a threat to Satan's kingdom.

It took us ten hours to drive the 620 miles before we arrived in Dallas–Fort Worth area, around 2:00 p.m. I wanted to drive a little further, but Tammy could see beyond my better judgment that I was getting tired. She said it was time to stop for the day. We stopped for lunch and found a Motel 6 where we stayed that evening. Later that evening, we went out to find something to eat. We found a Kentucky Fried Chicken for Tammy and me and a McDonald's for the kids. We then returned to our motel room to relax for the rest of the evening. I went to sleep around 8:00 p.m. to rest up for tomorrow's drive. Tammy and the kids watched TV until they all fell asleep.

We began the second day of our three-and-a-half-day journey by leaving the Dallas–Fort Worth area at 6:00 a.m. that morning. I drove for about two hours before I took my first break. We then started back on our journey, and I began my second lesson by studying the "Power Gifts of Faith, Healing, and the Working of Miracles." I started with _the gift of faith_ knowing that every Christian has a measure of faith, which in my opinion

169

is a gift that every believer has when they fully accept Christ as their Savior. The gift of faith is knowing full well that you are a child of God and that you believe what Philippians 4:13 says, "You can do all things through Christ who strengthens you," and realizing that you cannot accomplish anything spiritually on your own, but that our Lord has empowered you to move into new levels to do miracles and wonders in His name. The *gifts of healings*, which is the wondrous gift to use God's healing power to heal a person who is sick, injured, or have some type of difficulties in life. The healing gifts equip and allows the believer's hands and spoken word to be used as an instrument in various ways to pray for your own healing and to be used by believers to touch or speak the word of healing over someone's life. The *gift of working of miracles*, this spiritual gift is not manifested by human efforts but by the Holy Spirit. The work is unexplainable by nature. It edifies and delivers others. This gift is also used to display signs and miracles that give credibility to God's Word and to the Gospel message.

We drove another four hundred and eighty miles just outside Memphis, where we stopped for the evening. I finally got a chance to see Bishop Patterson's Temple of Deliverance Church of God in Christ Church located in Memphis. This was a beautiful church. I was glad that I got to see this church with my own eyes. The next day, or the third day of our trip, we left the Memphis area at 6:00 a.m. We drove 648 miles more through the rest of Tennessee, West Virginia, and parts of Virginia. We stopped that day in Roanoke, Virginia, for the third night of our trip.

My study lesson for the third day was the remaining nine gifts of the Spirit, which are the speaking gifts of the Spirit. They are speaking in tongues, interpretation of tongues, and the gift of prophecy.

I was amazed to learn that speaking in tongues was a gift. I always thought that every Christian had the ability to speak in tongues if they so choose to do so based on their denomination's beliefs and practice. The *gift of speaking in tongues* is a supernatural ability to speak and pray in a tongue or language that you do not know or fully understand. This comes flowing from within your spirit when you are talking, praying, or singing to God or used in a church service or gathering with other believers where God's anointing is flowing (1 Cor. 14:2, 13–14). I said to myself that I definitely have this gift.

The next gift that I studied is the *interpretation of tongues*. This gift is the ability to interpret the spiritual tongues that was spoken by you or another believer during a meeting or church service. The gift of interpreting tongues is a separate gift, but it seems to have been used in conjunction with the gift of speaking in tongues where God's anointing is flowing. The last gift that I studied was the *gift of Prophecy.* Believers with this gift typically have a strong biblical perspective and an ability to accurately proclaim God's Word. They are able to discern false doctrines and warn God's people about deception. A pastor, preacher, minister, teacher, or a prophet who declares the Bible truth can be considered as someone that speaks forth the word of God. I was glad that God gave me the opportunity to study these gifts of the Spirit during my trip home. Amen.

On the fourth day, we still had 436 miles left on our journey home. We had to finish driving through Virginia, Delaware, Pennsylvania, and through parts of New Jersey. We finally arrived in New Jersey, where we spent the next fifteen days staying over my mother's house, and then we left for Cleveland. We spent the next ten days in Cleveland. On August 15, it was time for us to head to Columbus. Columbus was only a two-and-a-half-hour drive from Cleveland. We were ready to begin our new life outside the Army. The first place that I wanted to visit was World Harvest Church so that we could figure out what section of Columbus that we were going to move too. Our plan was to move close to the church and Bible college. This was to cut down on the drive time to the school and church. Tammy's priority for our kids was to make sure whatever section of Columbus that we did move to have a good school system for our four kids to attend. We also wanted to make sure we would move to have a safe environment for our kids to grow up in. At this time, Tiesha was twelve, Chris was eleven, Latasha was ten, and Lloyd Jr. was five.

We arrived at the location on the map that said that we were at World Harvest Church. The building that we were looking at did not look like the typical community church that I was used to seeing, nor did it look like what I had envision in my mind for World Harvest Church. We were not sure if this building was in fact a church. It did have the appearance of something like a steeple on top. If this was the church, it was the biggest church that we have ever seen. There was farmland all around this area. I was not sure if this was even a church. The road sign that we just passed said we were on Shannon Road. I pulled off the road on the north side of this humongous property.

There was an older gentleman, whom I assumed was the groundskeeper, that was riding on a farm tractor lawnmower that was cutting the grass right in the area that we were parked. I guess he could tell that we were either lost or confused. He pulled his tractor alongside of my car where we were parked. He asked me if I needed help. I told him that I was looking for World Harvest Church and the Bible college. He laughed for a few seconds, then he smiled and said, "You are at the right place, but on the north side of the church's property. That is why you did not see the sign indicating that this was the church." He also said that the Bible college was located about two miles away. I thanked him for the information. He waved and said, "Have a blessed day," and continued with his grass- cutting assignment.

We then drove to the front parking lot of this church. There was a sign big as day in front of the church that said, "World Harvest Church." This was the first time that we saw a megachurch. We got out of the car in the parking lot to stretch our legs. You could feel the presence of the Holy Spirit just by walking around in the parking lot. I knew then that I was at the right place to learn more about God. I shouted, "Hallelujah! Praise the Lord!" We then proceeded to the hotel that we scheduled to stay at.

The following Sunday we attended the service. We were so moved by the service and the loving reception that we received that we joined the church. I was amazed when I found out, during our first church that we attended, that the nice gentleman that helped us was Pastor Parsley's father.

We decided to move into a townhouse in the city of Reynoldsburg, which is a suburb of Columbus. The drive to the church was less than five miles and seven miles to the Bible college. I enrolled into the Bible college's pastoral studies program by the end of the week. We heard that World Harvest had a youth football team called the Warriors that were looking for a few more football players and cheerleaders for their youth team. That was music to the ears of my daughter Tiesha and my son Christopher. Soon they both were plugged in to their Warriors football program. Tiesha became a friend with Pastor Parsley's daughter, Ashley, and she also became a cheerleader. My wife, Tammy, would help out as an assistant cheerleader coach. It was a special treat when Pastor Parsley attended the football games. He would cheer and be just as loud and, other times, louder than everyone else on the sideline and in the bleachers. You could tell that he was having a wonderful time watching the Warriors win every game. Pastor Parsley also had fun talking with everyone that would talk with him at the games.

Time to Find a Job

After we joined the church and my family was settled into our new townhouse, it was now time for me to find a job. My military retirement check was okay, but not enough to take care of my growing family. It was my second week in Columbus, when I heard that the Franklin County Veteran's Commission was having a job fair for veterans within the next two days. So I went, dressed in a suit and tie. I was armed with a brief case with several copies of my Army-prepared resume. It felt odd wearing a suit to the job fair and not in my Army uniform that I was accustomed to wearing for the past twenty years. The only time that I wore a suit was to church, weddings, and funerals. This was the first job interview that I have ever had to go on in my life. I joined the Army straight out of high school and never had to look for a job outside the Army since 1976.

I was impressed with all the representatives from several of the major companies that I interviewed with during the job fair. I had good interviews with these companies. Every one of their recruiters expressed an interest in hiring me right away. It seemed that most of the jobs that really sounded good and the ones that I was interested in doing were offering to pay me good money. They were all daytime jobs, between the hours of 8:00 a.m. to 4:00 p.m., and were all supervisorial or manager positions. My Army experience supervising as many as a hundred and ten soldiers and supervising in different job fields met the qualifications for all these jobs. The good thing about these jobs was that I required little or no training, but if I did accept any of these job, whatever training that I needed would have been provided by these companies as a part of the hiring agreement.

All these jobs had a starting salary between $30,000 and $40,000 per year as a start, plus good benefits. They were all tempting, but I had to say no. If I did accept any of these jobs, I would have to put going to Bible college on hold. My spirit reminded me that I was in Columbus to attend Bible college and this was God's will for my life. As a Bible college student, I could not accept any of these first-shift jobs because they would have interfered with my Bible college schedule.

The Franklin County Juvenile Detention Center was hiring for all three shifts. This was a government civil service job. They offered me a much-needed second shift job that I needed, plus the job will work better with my college schedule. The detention center had a starting pay of $10 an hour or roughly a starting salary of $19,000 a year. The thought of making $40,000 a year compared to the $19,000 was a no-brainer. It would had been perfect if at least one of these jobs would have been during my desired second shift, but they were not. The thought of making $40,000 a year and twice the amount the detention center was offering was very tempting. It became a battle in my mind between the spirit in me and my flesh. A battle between what God wanted me to do and what Satan was trying to prevent me from doing.

My spirit wanted Bible college, while my flesh wanted the higher- paying job with the more money that was now teasing my mind. Mentally, I was torn between the two. Spiritually, I was not. I had to pray hard and rebuke the enemy. Yes, God won this battle. Going to Bible college versus the temptation of the world was well worth the sacrifice. Even though my sacrifice of turning down this amount of money is no comparison to the sacrifice that Father Abraham was about to make in Genesis 22:8; nevertheless, I felt like Father Abraham when he told Isaac that God will provide.

My spirit reminded me at that moment that the $10 an hour was the amount that I asked God for during my last prayer in the El Paso desert. I quickly learned a valuable lesson that the cost of living in Columbus was much higher than living in El Paso. Making $10 an hour in Columbus,

Ohio, won't get you far. The two prayers that I prayed for before leaving El Paso became true. The Bible college acceptance was great, but the $10 an hour was going to hurt once I started receiving my paycheck from my new job. The Holy Spirit taught me a valuable lesson that you have to be careful about what you pray for because God does hear and answers your prayers if it is according to His will. Amen.

On September 1, 1996, I officially retired from the Army. By this time, I was an Army retiree, a Bible college student, and was scheduled to start my new job the following week as a detention center youth worker. During my first week of training at the detention center, I had to go through a one-day new employee orientation followed by a four-day classroom training program. My second week of training was considered hands-on training. I was allowed to work on the male housing unit, which is called a pod. I had to work alongside an experienced detention center worker who was responsible for my initial training. It was important that I worked alongside with an experience worker for my protection and safety. This was to give me some of the much-needed skills and some experience before I was allowed to work alone on these pods. I was glad to find out that most of the detention center workers claim to be Christians. It was not long before I found out that some of them never showed the love of Jesus or was patient with the youth. Matter of fact they were the worse in their treatment of the troubled youths.

Many of the youths were considered repeat offenders because they have been in the detention center numerous times within the past two years. As far as these repeat offenders was concerned, I was considered a rookie and new meat to them. They were wise and knew the detention center routine, and I did not. They also knew how to take advantage of a rookie detention center worker like me. The same youths would bully and would instigate the young, the weaker, and the first timer in the detention center to fight each other for their entertainment. Many of the newer youth were afraid to report the bullying to the staff because they were afraid of the retaliation from the bully's friends.

I quickly learned during my second week that many of these teenagers had serious alleged charges pending against them ranging from grand theft auto, burglaries, drug dealings, murders, and other gang-related crimes. The other teens had weapon charges pending. I was surprised and concerned when I found out that younger kids between the ages of ten and twelve were in this detention center because they were considered as high-risk runaways. Somehow the courts sent them to the detention center for their safety and protection. All the youths in this center were between the ages of ten and seventeen. Every one of them were allowed to sit with the general population with the eleven other youths during the hours of 6:30 a.m. until 8:00 p.m. when it was time for them to be placed in their individual cells to prepare for their medications and then bed. All the youths under my watch had still-pending court hearings and are innocent until proven guilty.

Every morning around 6:00 a.m., they would be awakened by the first-shift detention center youth worker to take showers, and then they were let out of their cells at 6:30 a.m. to attend breakfast, which were the first activity on their daily schedule. They would watch TV, play cards, argue among themselves, and start fights during my shift. My shift started every day at 2:30 p.m. This gave me time in the mornings and early afternoons to attend my Bible college classes and a brief time to complete my homework assignments. I had the responsibility for their protection and safety during my shift, which ended each evening at 10:30 p.m.

The only time that the youths could leave the pod as a group was for mealtimes, gym time, and for school classes that were conducted in classrooms in the detention center by Columbus public school- assigned teachers. The only

177

other times that the youths were allowed to leave the pods as individuals (with an escort) was during court appearances, family visits, or to attend church services inside the center. It was interesting how many of these youths would volunteer to attend church solely to get out of the pod. I would quietly pray for each youth that was on their way to church.

It did not take long before a fight would break out between rival gang members on many of my days when I worked alone. Many of these kids were between the ages of ten to seventeen years, and many of them were repeat offenders. Here I was locked up inside with them.

Later, on one of those days that I was working alone, an angry thirteen-year-old youth took a swing at me after I took away his playing cards because the other youth accused him of cheating and he was threatening to kill a teen on my pod. I had to call for back up to help me place the youth in his cell for a time-out and until he could be transferred to another pod because of his threat to kill another youth. God taught me a critical lesson that I had to treat all of them with the same love that I treated the youth that I had pastored at the AME Church in El Paso. It was good that I was a Bible college student. I was now using some of my training to show patients, humility, and express the love of God during demanding situations at the detention center. I soon started receiving respect from the youth on my pod after they realized that I was a minister and a Bible college student and I also showed that I was someone that really cared about them.

My spirit reminded me that when Jesus died on the cross, he did not do it just for me, but he did it for all of them too. My spirit also reminded me that every one of these kids had a praying mother, grandmother, granddad, a family member, or a church family that was praying for their safety and for these kids to turn their young lives around. Most of these kids had been in church. It was the socioeconomic environment and peer pressure that got them in the detention centers.

My spirit quickly reminded me that God had a purpose for me to be there. I learned that most of these kids came from broken homes or homes without a father figure. I also learned that they were following or beginning the incarceration path or the path of destruction that their fathers and other family members were traveling on. Many of the youth did not have a positive male role model in their lives and did not like to obey authority and would always try to challenge your authority. It was tough dealing with some of these youths, but I would ask myself all the time, especially during high stress and mentally challenging times, "What would Jesus do?" if He were doing this job. I would ask how would He turn these youths lives around.

After several weeks working with these youths, I realized that working at the juvenile detention center and being locked up inside with these youths gave me exceptional access to them that needed a role model and for someone that they could trust to talk to about their troubles and inner most feelings. This was a set up by God. Quietly, I started ministering to these youth. They started to enjoy my talks about Jesus and how they could turn their young lives around. Being that I was once an Army recruiter, many of them would also talk with me about careers in the military. This gave me another tool to explain to them the need to stay out of trouble and to stay in school and to graduate from high school and get that much-needed high school diploma if being in the military was one of their career choices.

I was thankful that God gave me this opportunity to be a lifeline to these youths. Even if it were to save a couple of the youths that were headed for a life of destruction. it was well worth the sacrifices that I had to make to stay in this job for a little while longer. My spirit said to me that by saving two or three of these youths per week and

179

planting the seeds of salvation in their hearts, I was saving several generations. I believed by faith that many of them changed their lives as a result of my interaction with them. I was proud that none of these youths that I worked with and ministered to ever returned to the detention center during the thirteen months that I worked at the detention center. Amen.

My Bible College Days

It was fantastic being a Bible college student at World Harvest Bible College's School of the Spirit. We had students not only from the United States but young men and women from many of the countries from around the world. All of us were spiritually hungry and proud to be a Bible student at World Harvest Bible College. Being at the Bible college was like being back in the Army's basic training again, but this time, I was preparing for battle against a different and more powerful enemy. Every day and every class that I attended was led by a spirit-filled instructor.

Sister Jolly, whom I loved so much, was my first-period English teacher. She would always start most of her classes by playing a song from Juanita Bynum's album *Morning Glory*. It was powerful listening to songs from Juanita's album like "Shake Us Again," "Morning Glory," and other songs from her album. We had a wonderful time being filled with the spirit studying of all subjects, English. By the time we left Sister Jolly's classroom each day, we were fired up for the rest of the day. I used to call her classroom a recharging station for a fresh anointing of my spirit. Amen.

I also had several other teachers like Elder Canfield, Elder Bender, and Mother Parsley who taught Bible college classes that deposited so much learning into my spirit. Every Monday morning, and sometimes during the other days of the week, we would start our Bible college mornings with a Spirit-filled chapel service. Elder Bender, Elder Canfield, and several other Bible college instructors would motivate us with their inspiring preaching and teaching during our chapel services. It was amazing and a blessing hearing and watching our instructors preach and lead by example. Every student would praise the Lord with our singing, shouting, and speaking in our heavenly language to the Lord. It was especially motivating when several of our fellow students were given the opportunity to preach while other students were given the opportunity to sing solos during the chapel service too.

World Harvest Church services on Sunday mornings and Sunday evenings was the perfect place to be for a Bible college student. I can remember the first time that I entered this marvelous sanctuary. I was blown away by the size of the congregation, TV cameras, and the wonderful spiritual atmosphere that was flowing. The first time that I saw Pastor Parsley preach in person and not on the TV was an electrifying experience. Every sermon that he preached was a mind- blowing lesson on the goodness and mercies of God. In a small way, I felt like Saul of Tarsus before he became the apostle Paul sitting under the feet of the Rabbi Gamaliel in Acts 22:3.

There were other Sundays that Pastor Parsley would invite and yield over his pulpit to other great and powerful men and women of God, and I could only wish that I could be in their presence and soak in their glory of their anointing too. Being a Bible college student and attending this anointed church gave me the blessing to be in the presence and to see with my own eyes and hear with my own ears and not on TV some of the greatest preachers of our times, like the great Norvel Hayes, Benny Hinn, R. W. Schambach, Reinhard Bonnke, Donnie McClurkin, Creflo Dollar, Darlene Bishop, Kenneth Copeland, Juanita Bynum, and special guests like NFL great Reggie White and many more that were invited to preach at our Sunday services.

It was a double blessing for us at the Bible college when many of these men and women of God would come and preach to us the following morning at our Monday morning chapel service. I could have never imagine listening up close to and shaking hands after their service with Donnie McClurkin, Darlene Bishop, Kenneth Copeland, Juanita Bynum, and many more. Each one of them blessed us with their impartation to each of our lives. Each time that they preached it turned into a Holy Ghost movement from God. Donnie McClurkin was the most serious, Kenneth Copeland was the funniest, and Juanita Bynum the most personable. She blessed me the most about stories about her personal life, her struggles, her relationship with men, and her funny story about how she was able to purchase a brand-new 1997 remake of the convertible Volkswagen beetle before anyone else could purchase the new model Beetle with no money down.

Going to World Harvest Bible College was not just about attending classes, chapel services, and homework. Every student had to be plugged in to a ministry at the church, which gave them hands-on and real-world experience ministering to souls outside the many walls of the Bible college and of this church. You had a choice to be in one of many powerful ministries that we were allowed to participate in like the kids and youth ministry, street ministry, prayer ministry, hospital and prison ministry, hospitality ministry, and many more. I felt led by the spirit to work in the prayer ministry during the two years that I was blessed to attend the Bible college.

When I would arrive for my prayer shift, the prayer room captain would meet me outside the prayer room prior to my entering to what I called the prayer chamber of healings and blessings to pray for me. The prayer captain would look at me to make sure that I was mentally and spiritually prepared for battle. Then they would pray and cover me with a hedge of protection and would empower my mind and spirit to represent Pastor Parsley's ministry in tearing Satan's kingdom down.

After the covering, I became an anointed and mighty man of God, prepared to do battle on these anointed prayer lines. When I left the presence of the anointed prayer captain, I would enter the prayer room feeling like Superman, or should I say like a Super Prayer warrior, coming out of a spiritual phone booth. I was covered by the blood of Jesus and protected with the whole armor of God from any counterattacks that could come from the enemy. I was now battle ready. Every time that I answered the phone as a battle-ready prayer warrior, I could feel the caller's spirits and sense the reason why they were calling before they could even speak a word.

When I prayed for each caller, I could feel the power of Pastor Parsley's anointing flowing through the phone. Strongholds were being broken, marriages were mending, generational curses were being destroyed, cancer cells and brain tumors were shrinking, and healings were happening in the caller's body, and their finances were being blessed if that was something that they needed too. Everyone that I prayed for would end the call shouting "Hallelujah" or "Praise the Lord, I am healed!" There were days that I could discern from several caller's voices that they were plagued by a demonic spirit. Of course, I prayed for the demonic spirit to depart. I could sense the release of the demon spirit and relief in the caller's voice when I shouted, *"Demon spirit, be gone in the name of Jesus!"*

One of these prayer calls was a frightening experience for me. It was from a female caller when she acknowledged that I was right in saying that she had a powerful and evil spirit that was running her life into the ground. She started crying and confessing that she was addicted to alcohol, drugs, and sex. She was now asking for the demon to be gone. We touched and agreed for her healing. When I shouted, *"Demon spirit, be gone in the name of Jesus,"* the caller drop the phone, and I could hear her convulsing and fighting with the evil spirit in the background. Suddenly, the phone was hung up.

Tears started flowing from my eyes when I realized that there was no way to call her back because she called in as an anonymous caller and did not give her phone number either. I was bothered by what I had experienced and was concerned about her spiritual safety. I prayed immediately for God to intervene and save the woman from this evil spirit. I gave it to God knowing that He would make this lady whole. Amen in Jesus's name.

The Holy Spirit Gave Me an Assignment

I attended World Harvest Bible College for two years and remained a member of the church to this day. I continued for several years after Bible college as a prayer warrior in the prayer center. Just around this same time, I was on one of my private time runs in the park, that the Holy Spirit spoke to my spirit about forming my own ministry. I learned that there were many ways that the good news can be spread. The Bible also says in 1 Corinthians 12:5 that there are differences of ministries but the same Lord. The Holy Spirit gave me a dream of a Roman road that was already built that extended from Jerusalem and went to every corners of the earth.

I found myself in my dream walking behind in the footsteps and path of the shadow of a spirit of a man from the early church that was carrying his cross hunched across the front of his left shoulder, which was held up by his left hand. He had strapped to his right hip a bottomless bag of seeds that he was reaching into and tossing them into the air with his right hand as he took each step. I followed in his footsteps that seemed like miles on top of miles. The odd thing about this dream was that the seeds were not touching the ground but were hovering in the air as if they were alive as harbingers of good news.

The Holy Spirit then spoke to my spirit. He said that I am that man, who was a representative for Christ, that was sowing those seeds. The seeds of the Great Commission and the Living Word of God were being sown into the air. The internet is the path that he wanted my ministry to travel on to spread the message of the Great Commission and the Word of God and that the cross is a sign to the world that I am a representative of Christ, who is no longer on the cross. Amen.

186

So, I was inspired by my dream to create an online ministry with the goal of reaching the saved, the unsaved, the backslider, and the unchurched and to remind the Christian world that we must remember Jesus's commandment about the Great Commission. I knew I had a God-ordained mission to spread the Good News, but I did not know at first how to begin. God gave me this dream and the authority to spread his message. He wanted me to act and take the next steps. It was now my time to develop a plan and put my dream into action. I prayed and fasted; and I did the research on ways to, first, create a name for my ministry; second, come up with a name for my website; and lastly, how to create an inspiring and creative Christian website. I gave my ministry the name of I Am for Christ Ministries, and I named my website as The Great Commission Pledge. I had to take all the necessary steps to get my ministry registered with the state of Ohio and to protect the ministry's name.

Next, I had to create and register my website and then create pages with messages about what the Holy Spirit wanted the world to hear from my site. These are messages that would advance God's kingdom. I was inspired to create five different pages at first with titles like "What Is Your Part in the Great Commission," "You Are an Ambassador for Christ," "A Message on Salvation," "The Ministry of the Holy Spirit," "How to Share your Faith." My idea to add YouTube teaching, preaching, and music videos helped me to explain my message better.

These videos that are from well-known ministries and music artist added credibility to my site, and they worked out perfectly with the written message that I wanted the world to know. The YouTube videos that I used were free on the web and there was no need to reinvent the wheel. I did put a line on my site thanking their ministries for making their work available for the world to see. It took me about a year of praying and fasting keeping my website in the draft mode so that no one else on the web could see the progress or the mistakes that I was making.

On July 25, 2015, my dream came to fruition and my challenging work was now starting to pay off. It was now the perfect time to launch my first international website ministry. The Great Commission Pledge https://www.tgcpledge.org/ was now on the Web and available for the entire world to see. It took about a year before I started seeing the fruits of my labor. Soon afterward, I received my first notifications on my "Message of Salvation" page that a person had turned her life around and had accepted Christ as her Savior.

I shouted, "Hallelujah," at the top of my lungs, and I did a praised dance like David did when I read the form of salvation that I placed on my page. Ten days later, I received another notification of salvation. I was happy for the two souls that accepted Christ. Since then, we average about twenty-five conversions per year that can be verified by the online form that is filled out by the new Christian, acknowledging their acceptance of Christ. I feel in my spirit and I know in my heart that many more have accepted Christ because of our labor. Amen.

Most of the believers would give their names and what state or country that they were from, while others would not; however, they did accept Christ anonymously, which was their right to do. It was important for us to know, and I was curious to know exactly where we were reaching souls for Christ. We also wanted to email them brochures on their salvation and their new life with Christ. I discovered that I could find out where by adding the Google analytics app to my website. This app allowed me to know in general where we were being reached in the United States and what foreign countries that we were reaching for our Savior.

I was amazed when I received my first report that we had viewers from every state in the United States and also in twenty-seven countries around the world. The Holy

Spirit whispered to my spirit that it was time for me to add another Google app called Google Language Translator to my site. The Google Language Translator app allowed my messages to be translated into 133 different languages around the world. Soon afterward, our reports were indicating that thirty-nine more countries were visiting our site for a total of sixty- three countries around the world.

As the pastor of this ministry, I was proud of our accomplishments.

I was then inspired by the Holy Spirit to write what is known by many as the Great Commission Pledge. (https://www.tgcpledge.org/the-great-commission-pledge).

THE GREAT COMMISSION PLEDGE

FIRST and most IMPORTANTLY,
I BELIEVE in the Father, the Son and the Holy Spirit
I ACCEPT the Bible as the inspired and only infallible and
authoritative written Word of God from *Genesis 1:1 thru Revelation 22:21*
I AM ONE of many MEMBERS of the Body of Christ
I ACKNOWLEDGE and CONFESS that I AM A SINNER saved by Grace
through faith *Ephesians 2:8*
I THANK God for his son Jesus who died on the cross for ME

I HAVE READ Jesus' last instructions to his disciples contained in the
Gospel of *Matthews 28:18-20*, known as

THE GREAT COMMISSION

Where Jesus said:
[18] "All authority has been given to Me in heaven and on earth. [19] Go
therefore and make disciples of all the nations, baptizing them in the name
of the Father and of the Son and of the Holy Spirit, [20] teaching them to
observe all things that I have commanded you; and lo, I am with you always,
even to the end of the age." Amen

I AM PROUD TO BE a BELIEVER and a DISCLIPLE of Christ
I ACCEPT MY calling and commission as an AMBASSADOR
for Christ *2 Corinthians 5:17-21*
I CAN DO all things through Christ who strengthen ME
I AM READY, WILLING, and ABLE.
I PLEDGE to do MY PART in the spreading of the Gospel

SO HELP ME GOD! AMEN

It was a blessing knowing that this pledge could also be translated into 133 different languages around the world.

I did a research paper in my evangelism class at World Harvest Bible College about ways to reach the 10/40 window one day. The internet was one of the ways that I included in my research report. My prayer now was that God could hopefully use my website platform to reach souls in the 10/40 window. The 10/40 window is the rectangular area of North Africa, the Middle East, and Asia approximately between ten degrees north and forty degrees north latitude. The 10/40 window is often called the Resistant Belt and includes the majority of the world's Muslims, Hindus, and Buddhists. The 10/40 window is home to some of the largest unreached people groups in the world such as the Shaikh, Yadava, Turks, Moroccan Arabs, Pashtun, Jat, and the Burmese people. These are also some of the poorest countries in the world. With this being said, I was hoping that some of them do have access to the internet by now. I prayed to the Holy Spirit to assist me in touching hearts and minds in this difficult region in the world. There was no doubt in my mind that we were going to reach souls in this area and that we were spreading Jesus's commandment about the Great Commission. Amen ("Joshua Project" www.joshuaproject.net).

On January 12, 2018, I began the second phase of my campaign in the war against the enemy. I was led by the Holy Spirit after the success of my first website to launch my second international website under the battle-ready banner of I Am for Christ Ministries (www.iamforchrist.org). Our mission this time is to provide resources and support to believers around the world that are working behind the scenes that are uplifting the name of Jesus. We also believe that every Christian should be able to boldly declare that "I Am for Christ." The declaration of using capital letters for "I Am" combined with the phrase "for Christ" is a powerful and double declaration of the sonship to the King of Glory and that you as a child of the King have limited powers and authorities to make a declaration. The addition of "for Christ" gives you the power and authority to represent the risen Son on this earth. The word *Christ* represents the Messiah who is also called the Anointed One and his anointing.

With all this being said, "I Am for Christ" is a declaration that you are a child of the King and that you have the authority of sonship to declare a thing that I Am (that) and to represent Christ here on earth. The Holy Spirit breathed into my spirit to write another slogan called "I Am for Christ Declaration." The purpose of this declaration is to inform the church world that it is okay to declare that "I Am for Christ" and that we have the authority and the power as a child of God to make the declaration that I Am (that). What you declare or what follows after I Am (that) become what you declared. Go to the webpage the Power of I Am to see your authority to declare I Am (that) what follows after you declare I Am (that) (https://www.iamforchrist.org/the-power-of-i-am/). Amen.

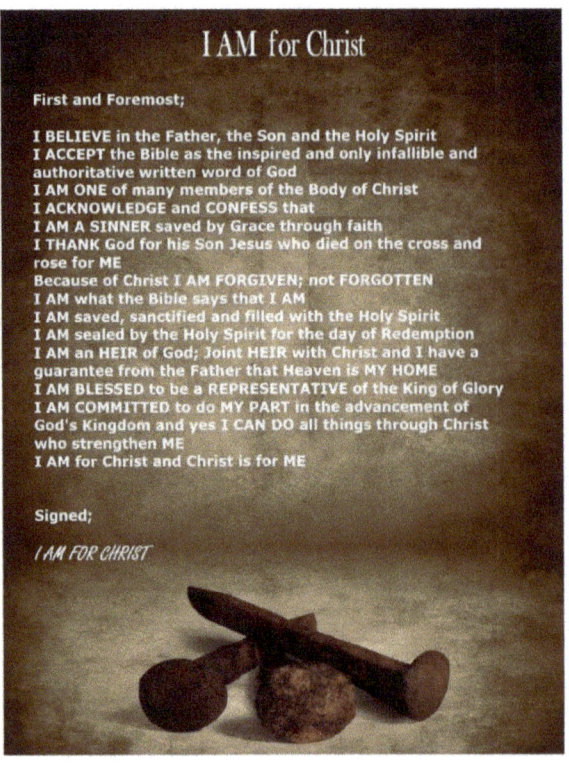

God has given me a worldwide mission and a vision to stand in agreement and to add our corporate faith to the faith of those believers that are working behind the scenes that are uplifting the mighty name of Jesus all around the world. God knows that there are so many dedicated believers of Christ that are laboring behind the scenes representing Him in churches, missions, ministries, homeless shelters, food pantries, foster homes, schools, day-care centers, prisons, barber and beauty shops, hospitals, sports, the military, Christian businesses and organizations, and every aspect of life. Many of them have answered the call to serve God's people as volunteers and generously giving up their time and, for many, their own finances. This inspired us to create and place on our website two different certificates with the titles "Representative of Christ" and "Ambassador for Christ." This came with small fee that only covered the cost of producing and shipping and handling of the certificate. The purpose of these certificates is to give the volunteer a certificate and a credential card just like what a minister has but without the privilege to conduct a marriage or to conduct a funeral service.

I Am for Christ Ministries Certificate Program *
https://www.iamforchrist.org/about-us/i-am-for-christ-certificate-program/

Representative's certificate

193

I am reminded by what Jesus said in Matthew 9:37–38 that "the harvest is truly plentiful, but the laborers are few. Therefore, pray the Lord of the Harvest to send out laborers to the harvest." The Apostle Paul in 2 Corinthians 5:20 called you an ambassador for Christ. There is no greater honor than one who laborers and represents the King of Glory. This alone is worth shouting about! Amen.

Every believer in Christ is a member of the body of Christ (1 Cor. 12:27). The Bible is clear that you and I have been given a divine assignment by God to do something to advance His kingdom. God has also equipped us with the desire, the anointing, and the Holy Spirit to guide us to be successful in whatever assignment God has blessed us to do for Him. We are in a battle against the enemy. Now is the time to put on your uniform, tie up your bootstrap, and to stand up to be counted as a warrior on the battlefield for Christ.

Are you for Christ, and are you ready to do something for His Kingdom?

God never said that you have to be perfect or full of fire. He is looking to add mighty men and women of faith that are not perfect but are willing to be perfect in Christ, especially those that are not afraid to stand up and do their part as His representative. The good news is that you have the authority and the help of the Holy Spirit to contribute your talents right where you are. The Bible makes it clear in 1 Corinthians 12:4–6 that we all have different spiritual gifts to serve the Lord. My point is that your gifts, talents, and a little bit of your time are needed to help us advance God's kingdom. It is not by accident that you are reading or hearing this command by God. God is calling you out to do something for his glory.

The Holy Spirit once asked me, "Are you for Christ, or are you against Me?"

I replied with a proud shout, "I Am for Christ. Hallelujah!"

So, I am asking you the same question now. Are you for Christ or are you against Him? If you can answer yes, I believe by faith that it would please the Father, the Son and the Holy Spirit to hear you say, shout, or do something in your own personal way with enthusiasm that "*I Am for Christ too. Hallelujah!*" If you have not already joined God's army before, we want to extend this opportunity to you now, and I want to be the first to welcome you as a soldier and laborer on God's team. Pray to the Lord of the Harvest that he shows you or
gives you a revelation to where you can be used in the vineyard for
Christ. Amen.

Having a Part in the Advancement of God's Kingdom

My experience working in ministry for many years has taught me that each one of us that believe in Jesus Christ has been given the power and the authority by the Holy Spirit to represent Jesus no matter where we live in the world or whatever is our life situation or station in life. Every one of us has a place and a position in God's vineyard. One of the simplest ways that we can do our part is to show kindness and the love of Jesus right where you are. You don't have to announce to the world that you are a follower of Christ. Your actions and how you conduct your day-to-day business, how you treat your fellow men and family members, and what you do when no one is looking are wonderful indications to whom you belong too.

There is nothing wrong with wearing a Christian hat or a sporting a Christian T-shirt that says, "I love Jesus" or "Jesus is my Rock and my Salvation." In reality, this is a public confession and a testament that you believe in Jesus and is one of the simplest ways that you can be used as a walking billboard to do your part in spreading the Good News. This is evangelism 101. People that you pass by do look at what you are wearing. Some pay attention, while others do not. You will never know if what you are silently preaching is planting a seed of hope, salvation, or joy into someone's spirit. It could be a lifeline that saves a soul from a life of destruction or even prevent a suicide. The gospel truth is that God wants to use you in whatever capacity that you feel comfortable with doing at first in the vineyard.

Let me give you another simple example: a high school football player that just scored a touchdown and kneels down. When he kneels down and gives God the victory sign, they are knowingly or unknowingly telling the crowd that they believe in God and that they are giving Him the victory for allowing them to score a touchdown. Can you think of any way that you spread the Good News knowingly or unknowingly? Start with doing something for God's kingdom with the purpose of giving God the glory, and this will allow God the pleasure of allowing you to do more. I challenge you to read or to remember what the apostle Paul said in 1 Corinthians 3:6–8 about planting and watering. It is God who will give you the increase to do more. Amen.

I have a special anointed T-shirt that I love wearing. It has my ministry's war banner on it. On the front of the T-shirt are the words "I Am for Christ Ministries" with a picture of a crown of thorns and two nails from the nailed hands of our crucified Savior. On the back of the T-shirt, the words say, "Jesus paid it all" with the cross of Calvary in the center of the shirt. I make it my duty to wear my special anointed T-shirt about everywhere I go, especially in crowded malls, family events, restaurants, and also in airports when traveling. My purpose of doing this is to make me a walking billboard for Jesus, and it gives me a large vineyard and avenue to silently but visually minister and to put seeds in their minds that Jesus is the one who paid it all for our salvation. Sometimes a get stares, but most of the time, I would get smiles from believers. They would say "I love your T-shirt" or "Amen, brother." I would interpret that they were really saying "I Am for Christ" too. Amen.

"I Am for Christ" T-shirt, front side

"I Am for Christ" T-shirt, back side

Let's be honest. Every person, regardless of age, with the exception of infants, in the United States and those in the civilized world have heard of the name of

198

Jesus, and about every one of them have said or thought something about the man named Jesus. We have to admit that this is no different from most of us having at times when we read, hear, or say something about the names of Buddha, Allah, or one of their spiritual gods. Yes, God is the creator of all of us. We must also realize that Christianity is not the only religion in the world. It is up to God to save those that have their beliefs in someone else other than Jesus the Christ.

Some of them had made the decision not to follow Jesus because they think that Jesus was a prophet and not the Son of God. It could be because of where they live and what they have been taught. It could also be because of the religion they have chosen, and for many, they don't have the choice because they live in a country that has forced state-sponsored religion. Yes, there are people who don't believe that there a God at all. The good thing about Christianity is that our big God gives us the choice to accept or not to accept His Son, Jesus, as our Savior. Let us not forget that there are citizens in the United States and civilized world that have heard the word of God and have not accepted Christ yet. There is also those that have tasted the gift of salvation but have turned their backs on Him for whatever personal reasons. Again, it is up to God to save whomever he chooses to save. Our mission is to encourage them and to offer them Jesus. Amen.

There is no doubt in my mind that every Muslim, Buddhist, Hindu, other beliefs, the atheist, and the unsaved had wondered and have had questions, either good or bad, about the man named Jesus. There is an exception: those that live in the 10/40 window. Again, it is my prayer that our ministry, I Am for Christ Ministries, is penetrating the atmosphere and is depositing the seeds of salvation into the hearts and minds of those that live in this difficult areas to reach. Right now, would be a suitable time to add your prayers to the prayers of all the saints around the world that are praying that the word of God is reaching every corner of this world. God breathed into my spirit to write another slogan called #ILoveJesusToo (https://www.iamforchrist.org/ilovejesustoo). This slogan hopes to reach the children of Father Abraham and tell them about the fact that we are all related and that Father Abraham can't be happy with what is going on today between the Abrahamic religions: Jews, Muslims, and the Christians. Amen.

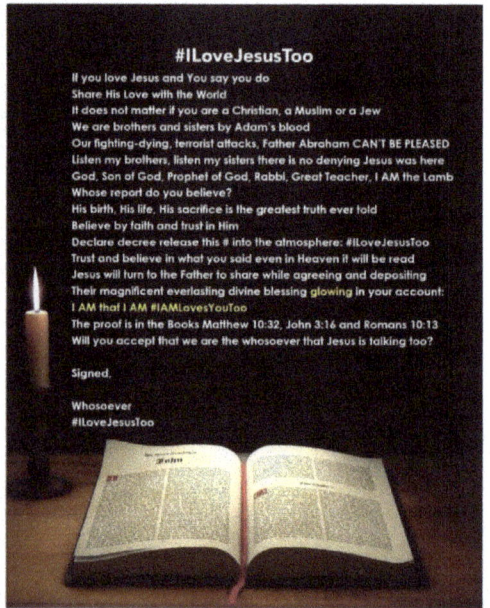

#ILoveJesusToo

I have always been proud to say that my ministry is a teaching ministry. It is my hope and prayer that we are, in fact, teaching, spreading the good news of the Great Commission and that we are changing lives for the glory of God. I stand on the words of the apostle Peter when he wrote these words at the inspiration of the Holy Spirit: "The Lord is not slow in keeping his promise, as some understand slowness. Instead, he is patient with you, not wanting anyone to perish, but everyone to come to repentance" (2 Pet. 3:9). This is my interpretation: God is patient but wants everyone to be saved. He knows that for some, it will take their whole lifetime before they accept Christ: our Christian faith, our beliefs, our acceptance of Jesus as our Savior, and our faith that the Bible are the words of God and that the Holy Spirit of God breathed on men to write the Holy Bible. We believe by faith that the Bible is the only road map that leads into heaven. Amen.

This is a word for my military brothers and sisters. How many of you remember singing the cadence to this motivational song during PT runs that said, "When I get to heaven. Saint Peter is going to say. How did you earn your living, how did you earn your pay and how did you get to heaven, boy? I replied with a whole lot of anger. Through blood, sex and a life of danger. I earned my living as an airborne ranger, Hoorah!" I am saying this to you today that singing the words of this song will not get any of us into heaven. Your acceptance of Christ and following the road map of the Bible is the only way. I am also positive that you are not going to meet St. Peter at the pearly gate either. You do have the promise that you will eventually see him in heaven. We all got to get there first. Hoorah and Amen!

The question is how do we get to heaven? I am glad you asked. It boils down to your acceptance of Christ and your relationship Him and others. Our God, who is the same Creator of heaven and earth, is also the one that we must stand before and give an account for what we did on earth. He is the one that will make the final judgment of all of us regardless of what religion or lack of religion that we chose. these judgments is for the saved, and the other is for the unsaved. You will only appear at one of these. God will determine which one that you will appear before Him. It is so important to read and

201

understand the difference between the two. I think that it would beneficial if you read on the judgment seat of Christ in 2 Corinthians 5:10:

> For we must all appear before the judgment seat of Christ, so that each of us may receive what is due us for the things done while in the body, whether good or bad.

The judgment seat of Christ is where you want to be when you have to give an account about your life to God. This judgment is for the saved in Christ or those that had truly accepted Christ as their Savior. This judgment does not determine your salvation; that was determined by Christ's sacrifice on the cross on our behalf. First John 2:2 (NIV) says, "He is the atoning sacrifice for our sins, and not only for ours but also for the sins of the whole world." All of our sins are forgiven, and we will never be condemned for them. We should not look at the judgment seat of Christ as God judging our sins, but rather as God rewarding us for our lives.

At the judgment seat of Christ, believers are rewarded based on how faithfully they served Christ (1 Cor. 9:4–27; 2 Tim. 2:5). Some of the things we might be judged on are how well we obeyed the Great Commission (Matt. 28:18–20), how victorious we were over sin (Rom. 6:1–4), and how well we controlled our tongues (James 3:1–9). The Bible speaks of believers receiving crowns for different things based on how faithfully they served Christ (1 Cor. 9:4–27; 2 Tim. 2:5). The various crowns are described in 2 Timothy 2:5, 2 Timothy 4:8, James 1:12, 1 Peter 5:4, and Revelation 2:10. James 1:12 is a good summary of how we should think about the judgment seat of Christ: "Blessed is the man who perseveres under trial, because when he has stood the test, he will receive the crown of life that God has promised to those who love him"

("What is the Judgment Seat of Christ/Bema Seat of Christ?" GotQuestions.org).

Now let us talk about what is called the great white throne judgment, which is also called the judgment of the unsaved. Let us read Revelation 20:11–15.

> Then I saw a great white throne and him who was seated on it. From his presence earth and sky fled away, and no place was found for them. And I saw the dead, great and small, standing before the throne, and books were opened. Then another book was opened, which is the book of life. And the dead were judged by what was written in the books, according to what they had done. And the sea gave up the dead who were in it, Death and Hades gave up the dead who were in them, and they were judged, each one of them, according to what they had done. Then Death and Hades were thrown into the lake of fire. This is the second death, the lake of fire. And if anyone's name was not found written in the book of life, he was thrown into the lake of fire.

The great white throne judgment is the final judgment prior to the lost being cast into the lake of fire. We know from Revelation 20:7–15 that this judgment will take place after the millennium and after Satan is thrown into the lake of fire where the beast and the false prophet are (Rev. 19:19–20, 20:7–10). The books that are opened (Rev. 20:12) contain records of everyone's deeds, whether they are good or evil, because God knows everything that has ever been said, done, or even thought. And He will reward or punish each one accordingly (Ps. 28:4, 62:12; Rom. 2:6; Rev. 2:23, 18:6, 22:12).

Also at this time, another book is opened called the book of life (Rev. 20:12). It is this book that determines whether a person will inherit eternal life with God or receive everlasting punishment in the lake of fire. Although Christians are held accountable for their actions, they are forgiven in Christ and their names were written in the "book of life from the creation of the world" (Rev. 17:8). We also know from Scripture that it is at this judgment when the dead will be "judged according to what they had done" (Rev. 20:12) and that "anyone's name" that is not "found written in the book of life" will be "thrown into the lake of fire" (Rev. 20:15).

The fact that there is going to be a final judgment for all men, both believers and unbelievers, is clearly confirmed in many passages of Scripture. Every person will one day stand before Christ and be judged for his or her deeds. While it is truly clear that the great white throne judgment is the final judgment, Christians disagree on how it relates to the other judgments mentioned in the Bible, specifically who will be judged at the great white throne judgment ("What is the Judgment Seat of Christ/Bema Seat of Christ?" GotQuestions.org).

My Final Points

Last I heard, it takes the Holy Spirit, who is the agent of salvation, to convict someone of their sins and to save them. We are only the earthly instruments that God uses to inspire or to lead someone to Christ. I have also learned that the four walls of a church building and the anointing of ministers and traveling missionaries are not the only ways that God can use to call, bless, feed, and save his people. The gospel truth is that God wants to use all of us and our God-given talents to reach and encourage people around the world to accept Jesus as their Lord and Savior. That is what the Great Commission is all about. We can all do our part with the help of the Holy Spirit. Amen.

We as human beings are finite beings while God, who is our creator, is infinite. This means that we are limited in our thinking and what we can imagine and do while God is not. He is limitless. Do not forget that God is the One that spoke the world into existence. He is the one who place the sky, stars, the moons, and galaxies in their proper positions; and He is the same One that sent his Son, Jesus, to be that sacrificial Lamb and became the Savior of the world. So, the question is, why do we keep putting God in a box? God, if He wants to, can save not only the Christian, but also the Muslims, the Jews, the Hindus, or anyone else that He chooses to save. If you are not aware of this, know that we live in the time period that is called the dispensation of grace. Remember that God is infinite and He is perfect in His ways. He desires your highest praise. Hallelujah!

God is the Righteous Judge, not us. We cannot judge anyone. We have no say so on who He will allow into heaven. This is not the Bible but me trying to make the following point. Can you imagine standing with St. Peter at the pearly gates, or heaven's gate, when someone arrives in heaven who you knew on earth as a big sinner or a believer from a different religious faith but was eventually saved by the grace and the mercies of God. You stop them before they enter in, and you tell St. Peter and God that in your opinion this person is not worthy to enter into heaven's gate. Do you think God will listen to you? Of course not. If you did, there will surely be weeping and gnashing of teeth. It will be you that will be weeping and your teeth that will be gnashing when your butt is being tossed out of heaven.

I am glad knowing and I have the assurance from the Holy Spirit that most of you that are reading my story have already accepted the call of salvation and are living the life as a saved Christian. I am also glad that many of you have answered the call of being a part of the fivefold ministry as an apostle, prophet, evangelist, pastor, or teacher, and for those that have answered the call as a missionary, going to places around the world, spreading the news of the Great Commission. I am also glad that many of you that are either paid workers or are volunteers working behind the scenes that are uplifting the name of Jesus in the vineyard and are an ambassador and representative for Christ. I also want to give a timeless special shout out to all those brothers and sisters that have answered the call to serve in our government and in our great military. Bless you and thank you all for your services to our nation. Amen.

Here is a hard truth. Please don't misunderstand what I am about to say. But it is really the truth. The life of a Christian is not all roses; a life filled with endless blessings or life full of answered prayers. Of course not. We are subject to the same potential tragedies, sicknesses, and disappointments that everyone in this life could potentially face as well. We all face the same cycles of life. We are all born from the womb of our mothers. We live our life for a period of time. The Bible does say that our lives are like a vapor. We are here today, gone today. Our life story is recorded in the Books of Life, and we will die according to God's perfect or permissible will for our lives,

206

and hopefully, our clay bodies are destined to be placed into the earth to await the day of judgment.

Depending on your denominational theology, doctrine, philosophy, or the lack of not having one of them, our spirits and souls must go somewhere into eternity to face either the reward or punishment of all three. That is your body, your soul, and your spirit. And finally, we will all have to give an account of what we did on this earth. Let me make this point clear and personal. The day of judgment is no longer about us, but about the you, or I, that must stand before the Master and give a personal account of what you, or I, did or did not do prior to taking our last breath on this earth: accepting or denying Christ as your Savior.

This is where we separate at our acceptance or denial of Christ. Please don't miss this. It is that important to emphasize this again. We that accept Jesus as our Savior are saved by His grace and mercy. We will go to the judgment seat of Christ already judged about our salvation. We will receive our rewards, but those that have denied Him are the unsaved. The unsaved will go to the great white throne judgment and stand in a long line with the great and the small. When it is time for the unsaved to give an account, they won't be able to lie, tap dance, or ask for someone standing nearby to tell God that you were a good person. The book of your life story will quickly flash before you like a sad movie, and you will not be able to mumble a single word in your defense especially at the missed moments of salvation when you could have said yes to Christ. The Bible truth is that good people don't make it into heaven, only the good that are saved and believe in Christ do! Only God, who is the righteous Judge, will determine where you or I will spend our eternity. Amen.

The Bible is clear that for some there will be a celebration and the reward of crowns and for others there will be gnashing of the teeth and the pain of punishment. The good thing about many of us is that we are saved by God's grace and mercy and we have our Lord and Savor Jesus, the anointed one, and His anointing. For He is our soon and coming King. We are sealed for the day of redemption, and we have fire insurance from the Father that heaven is going to be our home and not hell below.

My prayer is hopefully by now you should be able to know where you will stand before the Master and where you are going to give an account of your life's story. The question for you based on what you know now. Do you have traveling reservations to the judgment seat of Christ or do you have reservations to the great white throne judgment? If your answer is that you believe the great white throne judgment is where you are headed, you can start right now to get it right. Remember that tomorrow is not promised to no one.

Let me say that I have had my share of tragedies, sickness, and disappointments too. I feel led by the Holy Spirit to share my testimony. The recent passing of my beloved mother and a gifted prayer warrior, Eva Joann Glover; my beloved father-in-law, George Bland; my sister-in-law Patty Bland; and the passing of my beloved brother, Isaac Glover, hurt me the most. But I can rejoice that I have the promise from the Holy Spirit that heaven is now their home. Several years ago, I had to have two back surgeries that prevented me from enjoying my outdoor private time with God. It took the gifted and anointed hands of a surgeon to make me whole. I can now run, walk, and enjoy my outdoor private time with God again.

Four years ago, in December 2018, I had prostate cancer, but now I am healed while others I knew with prostate cancer died from it. Two years ago in January 2020, I suffered a disabling stroke; but through physical, occupational, speech therapy, and the mercies of God, I am on the road to full recovery and can now finish the assignment that God has given me to finish my life's story. As you can see, the devil tried to take me out several times, but the victory belongs to Jesus. Hallelujah.

On March 13, 2022, I participated in the Arnold's Annual Fitness Classic at Columbus, Ohio. This is a big event that occurs every year in Columbus that Arnold Schwarzenegger created and sponsors. Athletes from all over the United States participate in this event to compete in professional bodybuilding, weight lifting, cheerleading, and so many more world-class events. I participated in the 5K race that had an average age range of eighteen to seventy-two.

Many of the runners that participated in this race were professional milers, and many were marathon runners. Being that it was the winter months in Ohio, it was cold and wet. I really did not have clear weather to prepare for the race. I ran anyway. I was determined that there was nothing or no way that the enemy was going to stop me from competing. My goal was not to win it, but to be in it. I ran on behalf of disabled veterans, cancer and stroke survivors, and as a healed man of God, which I am all four. I wanted to give God the victory and the glory that I was even able to compete.

I spoke in tongues and prayed for all the runners that participated with me during the whole race. The whole race was mostly up a slight incline. I was proud of myself because I never stop running, considering this was the first time that I had ran more than a mile in the past six months. It was amazing seeing and hearing the crowd of spectators that were lined up cheering for me as I came close to the finish line. This motivated me to sprint the last hundred meters to the finish line. It felt really good and worth the pain running when I was presented with an Arnold Fitness Classic medallion for finishing the race. A 5K or five-kilometer race is a 3.1-mile race. My runtime was 11:18 seconds per mile. I finished two hundred and thirtieth out of six hundred plus participants. Not bad for a sixty-four-year-old man of God who had two back surgeries, a cancer and stroke survivor, and a retiree from the Army twenty-six years ago

(September 1, 1996). I ran with the healings and blessings from our God. Hoorah and hallelujah. Amen.

After the Arnold Fitness 5K race

This is worth repeating. We all face the same cycle of life. We are born to a woman, we are blessed to live for a period of time, we die, and hopefully, our clay bodies are placed in the earth to await the day of judgment. Depending on your denomination, theology, or lack of one, our spirits and souls must go somewhere into eternity to face either the reward or punishment for all three: your body, your spirit, and your soul. The Bible also says that for some there will be a celebration and for others there will be weeping and gnashing of the teeth. The question is, what judgment will you face? Amen.

Let us pray:

Holy Spirit, I bless your holy name, and I thank you for your guidance and words that are contained in this book. Bless those that are already believers and are already sealed for the day of redemption. I thank you in advance that we are heaven bound. I pray that lives were changed and that people have accepted your call of salvation all over the world. Motivate those that have not accepted your gift of salvation as of today. I ask you to open up their hearts and minds that they do so at the end of this prayer and before it is too late. Your Word say that tomorrow is promised to no one.

I also pray for encouragement to those that are sitting on the sidelines. Speak to their hearts and minds that they too are called to be an ambassador and a representative of your Son, Jesus. Father, I ask that you speak into their hearing that they too have a place in the vineyard to do something for the advancement of your glory. I love you and thank you in the saving name of your Son, Jesus. This is my prayer. Amen.

Saving souls for God's kingdom is what our teaching ministry, the Great Commission, and this book is all about. Our bottom-line mission is saving souls for God's kingdom. If you have not already or you would like to return to your first love, now is the moment. Today is your day, and this is your time and a perfect opportunity to ask Jesus to come into or back into your live. If you are ready, I ask that
you recite the prayer of salvation and let God do the rest. Amen.

The Prayer of Salvation

Dear Lord Jesus,

I know that I have sinned and I am a sinner. I ask for your forgiveness. I believe you died on the cross for my sins and rose three days later from the dead. I turn from my sins and invite you to come into my heart and my life. I want to trust and follow you as my Lord and Savior for the rest of my life. I ask this in Your Precious Name. Amen.

If you just said the prayer of salvation and you truly meant what you said, you are now saved by the grace and mercies of God and you are sealed for the day of judgment. You have the Holy Spirit's promise that heaven is going to be your home. We love you at I Am for Christ Ministries. Welcome, or welcome back, to the family of God. Please find a local Bible-believing church that is preaching and teaching the Gospel of Jesus Christ. Amen.

A Fresh and Double-Double Anointing Is Coming Your Way

Let me close out this chapter in my life story. I was having a tough time deciding on how I was going to end this book. I prayed numerous times to the Holy Spirit during the past three weeks for guidance. The Holy Spirit, who is my coauthor on my life story, did not answer my prayers on helping me to find a perfect closing message to end this book. He never did answer me. On August 25, 2022, I was having my weekly promised thank-you dinner to my wife Tammy at an O'Charley's restaurant in Canal Winchester, Ohio.

It has been thirty-one years ago since I made this promise to Tammy at the end of the Gulf War that I would take her to dinner every week for her support, love, and how she took loving care of my kids during my absence during the war. This was a promise that I kept except during my recovery time after my stroke. My nine-year-old grandson, whom I call my best friend and my special son, Tieson Glover, was with us. We have been blessed to have Tieson in our lives.

It was by coincidence that at the moment that I finished blessing our food, I started thinking about Sister Jolly and how much she and all of my instructors at World Harvest Bible College and the ministry of Pastor Rod Parsley had blessed my life and my ministry. I thought about her English class and how I used to call her classroom a recharging station for the anointing of my spirit.

I then noticed two elegantly dressed older ladies that had just finish their meal and were preparing to leave the restaurant. I thought for a minute that one of these ladies looked just like my favorite Bible school teacher, Sister Jolly, but I was not 100 percent sure. I hadn't seen

213

her in several years and the distance made it hard to tell. The two ladies walked down the aisle that was the closest to our table. The spirit in me started jumping for joy when I noticed it was, in fact, Sister Jolly. I could not help myself, and I shouted out Sister Jolly's name loud. She turned and looked over toward me—and so did everyone else that was sitting nearby. She softly shouted my name, "Lloyd Glover," with a happy tone. Sister Jolly was surprised and glad to see me too. I got up and walked over to Sister Jolly. Despite Covid, we smiled, hugged, and said it was good seeing each other again.

I felt a jolt of energy that shot through my body as we hugged. We spoke for a minute, then we said our goodbyes. Sister Jolly and her friend departed the restaurant. The spirit in me knew that I just received a strong and fresh anointing simply from her hug. I returned to my table. Tammy could tell that something was different about me. She asked me if I was okay. I told Tammy that I was fine, that I just need a second to catch my breath.

We finished our meal, and we went back home. I was so excited about my encounter with Sister Jolly that I played Juanita Bynum's songs "Shake Us Again" and "Like a Dew" as soon as I got home. These were two of the songs that Sister Jolly played for us in her classroom that energized every student in her English class for the rest of the day. Later that evening, prior to going to bed, I could still feel the fresh anointing that I got from the hug of Sister Jolly.

The next morning, I got up early as always. I went to my prayer closet thinking about the fresh anointing that I received from Sister Jolly the day before. I invited the Holy Spirit into my prayer closet like I would do every morning. I would pray and meditate with the expectation of hearing a word from God. I often play Juanita Bynum's song "Morning Glory" to get me charged up for the battle ahead of tearing down Satan's kingdom brick by brick. This is my daily goal. There were days that I could feel the awesome presence of the Holy Spirit that would engulf my prayer closet while I play the "Morning Glory" song. I felt it in my spirit that He, being the Holy Spirit, was enjoying Juanita's song "Morning Glory" too. And He seemed to also enjoy spending my private time with me. Amen.

Just prior to ending my private time with God that morning, I started reminiscing about my Bible college days being back in Sister Jolly's English class. My spirit told me to play Juanita Bynum's song that Sister Jolly would play for us at the beginning of class, "Shake Us Again." I felt a warm breeze like I did when I was healed from pulmonary sarcoidosis in the El Paso desert. My spirit could sense the presence of the Holy Spirit. I could sense His smile, and I could also detect His sense of humor when he spoke to my spirit: "We have been waiting for this day, so that you could receive a fresh anointing from your Sister Jolly. We wanted to first reward you for your faithfulness. We know how much you love our daughter and your sister Jolly and how her teachings have inspired you even to this day. We loved how you called her classroom a recharging station for the anointing of your spirit."

Yesterday when you saw Sister Jolly, it was no accident. It was a divine set up by Us to answer your prayers about a closing message for your wonderful book. Lloyd, my son, you are a gifted and an anointed teacher just like your sister Jolly, and just like Sister Jolly, you also have something to share with my children. We anointed Sister Jolly, and We gave her this assignment as our anointed vessel to give you a double-double portion of the anointing. And yes, you have our blessings to name your closing chapter as "A Fresh and Double-Double Portion of the Anointing Is Coming Your Way."

The Holy Spirit ended our encounter by saying, "We love your book, and we can't wait for the sequel. And by the way, my son, we have increased your territories; and we have another assignment for you. You will receive it in due time."

The End

215

About the Author

Lloyd C. Glover spent twenty years in the United States Army before retiring as a sergeant first class on September 1, 1996. He started his career as a Nike Hercules crewmen, then an Army recruiter, where he earned next to the highest recruiting award of three sapphires to the gold recruiting badge. He later served as a Patriot missiles senior sergeant serving in combat tours to Israel and Saudi Arabia during the Gulf War. He also served as the chief instructor over the Patriot missile training course at Fort Bliss, Texas, before his retirement. Lloyd is an ordained minister, a former youth pastor, and now the founder and pastor of two international websites and an online Bible training center. Lloyd attended World Harvest Bible College.

He grew up in Plainfield, New Jersey, during the sixties and seventies. This was a time of racial unrest and tensions in the United States. The Vietnam War was going on, and he was a witness when life in the United States for all nationalities was improving.

He is happily married to his wife, Tammy (Bland) Glover, of forty two years. They have four adult children, eight grandkids, and two great-granddaughters

216

and grandson. He is proud that two of his children followed in his military footsteps. His daughter Tiesha is an Air Force veteran, and his son Christopher Emmanuel is currently serving in the Navy as a chief petty officer.